FINDING OUR WAY HOME

A family's story of life, love and loss

by J Damon Dagnone

TABLE OF CONTENTS

Dear Damon and Trisha,

Thank you for this book. It is hard to know what is right or wrong to say since this is obviously such an intimate account of your life. It is brave, raw, and so very sweet. I cried pretty hard while reading it, but there were some happy tears too. Despite there being so little control in many things in life, it is nice to know something as simple as a popsicle, or a brother's love, shows you why there is always hope for good and laughter even in times of sorrow. It is an incredible honour to be part of your story, especially if I could have made even a small moment slightly more bearable. Would it be too much if I told you some of the stories I remember?

Do you remember the time you saw me in the ED in a bright orange hoodie and orange crocs? I loved that outfit when I was on-call. So comfy. You told me you loved it too, and so would Callum, because orange was his favourite colour. I wore it almost every call shift from then on and I wore it the night before my Royal College exams, during my written exam, and had it in my bag during my OSCE. I kinda felt like Callum could back me up, you know? Residency can be a grueling experience at the best of times and connecting with a family, and especially a child, makes it all worthwhile. Thank you for the raw descriptions of writing an exam even when you wanted to run screaming for the hills. I had some of my own tragedy around that time, although minor in comparison, and keeping focused was impossible so I thank my lucky stars everything worked out.

Do you remember the time you had me and Amy over for dinner? It was right before I moved away after my residency training. I remember looking at large framed paintings by your kids on the walls of your dining room, a place of honour, I suspect. I remember feeling a bit like an imposter because you had given me this award that had totally blown my mind and meant so much to me. You and Trish were hurting so badly and yet had the space to thank people and make other people feel special. Your entire family operates this way, I think. I received so many cards of thanks and congratulations after you offered me the inaugural award in Callum's' name. Your Dad sent me a note, on behalf of your whole family, thanking me as well. I think it was a time where you realize everyone is human, everyone is vulnerable, and to have your Dad reach out was pretty amazing.

Sometimes I find myself speaking like Trisha in some scenarios. I love Trish's voice. I hope she takes this as a compliment. She has this certain intention and speed to her voice that is sweet but means business. Maybe I use it a lot. It works. Thanks Trish (imitation is the highest form of flattery). Damon, you are an amazing physician and role model and I cannot wait to see your name in lights after the education curriculum you are working on (and this book) is published. I have so much love for you all and wish I knew Thai and Mae better as they are undoubtedly wonderful.

Thank you for the parts of this book that make me want to be a better parent. "What we do for our kids should be our Gospel." I say an amen to that. As a healthcare educator myself, I would like to see students in healthcare fields read this book, particularly those in pediatric training programs, oncology, and palliative care. To learn the lived experience of a family is a special gift and may serve to evolve our care to be better in the future!

Thank you for the reminder of Callum, whose picture is in my office, as part of the framed award you gave me. It is above my door on the inside and can only be seen if you come into my office and sit on the couch. Those people who come in always ask about this beautiful little boy. Sometimes before they read the page, they ask if it is Eddie, my guy. I love getting the chance to tell a little story about an ambulance ride one night that changed a piece of me.

I love thinking about your family and appreciate so much how you actually helped me understand my own family. Do you remember the singular reason I did pediatrics was because we lost my aunt's son (my fourth and only male cousin in our small family) to medulloblastoma in 1998? A similar story but without the path-of-healing part. My family has never been the same, and although they can speak somewhat of that time now, they turned inward almost absolutely and have not been able to continuing living in the same way as you and Trish. I only mention that because I tell parents all the time, they do not need to apologize for allowing laughter and hope back in their lives. Our children near and far would expect nothing less.

Please use my name in the book because I am so proud to know your beautiful family. I'm glad to know that we helped you and Trisha in many ways when we took care of you and Callum, because we were nervous that we weren't saying the right thing, probably didn't say the right thing very often, cried with you, and cried alone behind closed doors too.

I hope to see you soon.
Love always.
Sarah
General Pediatrician and Friend Forever
Head Pediatrics, Dalhousie Medicine New Brunswick

CHAPTER 1

Life Has Changed Forever

In the spring of 2006, I had just celebrated my thirty-third birthday and life was pretty great. The flowers and trees were blooming, the kids were outside playing with their friends, my residency in Emergency Medicine was nearing completion, and we were off to Disney World for our first family vacation. It was apparent to my wife Trisha and me that we had everything we could ever want. Our boys – four-year-old Thai and two-year-old Callum – were our pride and joy.

To say our vacation was the trip of a lifetime would be an understatement. The kids had such a good time just getting there – riding in the shuttle bus, going up and down the airport escalators, flying on the plane, then taking the tramway train and the express bus to Disney World – that once we reached the gates and they saw the giant images of Mickey and Minnie Mouse, Callum said, "Daddy, is it time to go home now? I've had so much fun!"

We had a perfect week seeing all the Disney characters and visiting the pavilions, riding the spinning teacups, buying overpriced balloons, eating popsicles and ice cream, and swimming in the endless number of pools at our hotel. Our trip was truly magical, except for the three occasions when Callum vomited for no apparent reason. The first time was in a restaurant in the Magic Kingdom, before dinner. The second was a few days later, right after we met Mary Poppins and Cinderella at breakfast. The third was at the end of our trip, in the Toronto airport. After the third episode Trisha and I were scared, Trisha even more than me as mothers generally have the best instincts when something is wrong with their child.

In the previous six months, Callum hadn't gained any weight despite having what we thought was a good appetite and his usual energy. Prior to Disney World, because we were concerned about his weight, he had undergone a number of medical tests for celiac disease, cystic fibrosis, and other medical conditions. The results came back normal. As a medical doctor, I tried to suppress thoughts that something more worrisome was going on. I tried to convince myself that his vomiting was due to something simple. I didn't want to think of the worst things it could be, like a metabolic disorder, a bowel disease, or scariest of all, cancer.

One week later Trisha phoned me to say she was en route to Kingston General Hospital because Callum couldn't stop vomiting. He seemed much more tired than usual, she said, but he didn't appear to be sick in any other way – no fever, diarrhea, or headache. Still hoping nothing was seriously wrong, I thought maybe Trisha's haste was premature, but once I arrived at the hospital, I too became very worried. After speaking with the on-call pediatrician, we all agreed Callum should be admitted for further workup and observation, despite the fact that the results of his X-rays, ultrasound, urine testing, and blood work that day didn't show significant abnormalities. Eventually, Callum was admitted to the pediatric ward, where I had previously cared for other parents' children during my pediatric training.

From the moment we arrived at the hospital that Friday, Callum was a perfect patient. He was happy, sociable, said thank you for everything, and was content to hang out with Mommy and Daddy reading books and playing Sesame Street on the computer. Later in the evening, Trisha went home to be with Thai and I stayed with Callum. I cherish that first night, when he and I had a sleepover in his bed on the pediatric ward.

Over the weekend a number of doctors came to see us. We discussed Callum's poor weight gain in the preceding months and the increased episodes of vomiting with no other symptoms. It seemed surreal that only one week ago, Callum was running around at Disney World, swimming, playing, laughing, wrestling, and sleeping beside his older brother. On the third day in hospital, Callum was visited by physicians from the gastroenterology service who were hopeful they could put the pieces together to explain his symptoms. A CT scan had been arranged for mid-afternoon to rule out the rare possibility of increased pressure around the brain.

Following Callum's CT scan, I hurried down to the radiology suite to review the images with the neuroradiologist, but I never made it. Halfway there, Callum's pediatrician stopped me in the hallway. Few words were spoken. I don't clearly remember what he said, but it didn't matter because I recognized the ominous look on his face, which told me that we needed to talk in a private area. I found Trisha and we went into the conference room, where we were told "Callum has a brain tumour." Our hearts stopped and life changed forever.

CHAPTER 2

The Diagnosis

The pediatrician's words reverberated through our minds. The two hours that ensued are difficult to describe. We felt shock, pain, anguish, and grief as we struggled to process our new reality. The absolute fear we felt was completely disabling. I remember Trisha and me standing in the middle of the pediatric ward, sobbing. It was every parent's worst nightmare.

And yet, despite the highly emotional circumstances, we were forced to think clearly so we could mobilize every resource we had to help us with what was to come. The multitude of actions that needed to take place in an urgent manner was staggering. This still didn't feel real, but there we were sitting in the hallway, crying, talking, and frantically planning while physicians, nurses, and other parents came and went on the ward.

Once before, when I was a medical student, I'd been part of a pediatric team that broke bad news (which I now understand was tragic news) to the parents of an unwell child. I was part of the hospital in-patient unit responsible for the assessment, admission, and care of this small boy. He was very cute and happy, despite being unwell, and I admired his mom and dad. They were a sweet couple and were very kind to me as a junior member of the team. They were especially grateful that I'd entertained their three-year-old when they had to briefly step out of his room. The next day, I was with the pediatrician when he told the parents their child had a rare form of leukemia. The proposed treatment would involve aggressive chemotherapy, radiation, and possibly a bone marrow transplant. I wasn't a parent then, but the grief and panic I witnessed on the faces of that couple shook me to my core. Now Trisha and I were living a similar story.

Many events occurred in the hours following Callum's diagnosis. He went for an emergency MRI of his brain. A referral was made to the Hospital for Sick Children (Sick Kids) in Toronto and Callum was to be urgently transferred by ambulance. A pediatric neurosurgeon at Sick Kids, Dr. Jim Rutka, was consulted. While we waited, the hospital's pediatric hematology-oncology specialist, Dr. Mariana Silva, came to introduce herself and prepare us for the next twenty-four to seventy-two hours. Trisha and I arranged for everyone in our family to be told and we tried to sort out how to make our other son, Thai, understand why we had to suddenly leave him with Nana and Papa for a few days. We had never both been away from him before, except the night Callum was born. We coordinated how at a moment's notice we would move to Sick Kids indefinitely.

Hours later, as I climbed into the ambulance with Callum, the paramedics, and Dr. Sarah Gander, Kingston General's senior pediatric resident, Trisha was speeding home to pack our things, say goodbye to Thai, and then drive to meet us in Toronto. Our lives had suddenly been shattered. We didn't have time to contemplate what lay before us. All we could think about was the next few hours. We'd deal with the next few days as they came.

Before I knew it, we arrived at Sick Kids. It was a little before midnight. We made our way via ambulance stretcher to a room on the neurosurgical ward. Minutes later, Trisha and my younger brother Vico arrived. We were full of fear and panic, while Callum was calm and content. He happily climbed from the ambulance stretcher into his new bed, said hi to the nurse, and then easily went to sleep. Trisha told me she'd given Thai her charm bracelet so he'd have something of Mommy's while we were in Toronto. After hearing that Thai was okay, we cried together and held each other. We then curled up on the little bench in Callum's room and managed to fall asleep, continuing to hold each other tight.

The first few days at Sick Kids involved meeting many new people: the neurosurgical team, the neurosurgeon, the hematology-oncology team, the social worker, the child-life workers, and the numerous nurses and other healthcare professionals responsible for Callum's care.

We were at the mercy of everyone involved in organizing the surgery to remove his tumour. We could think no further than how soon the tumour could be taken out, how dangerous the surgery would be, what the potential complications for Callum could be, and if there was any possibility for a cure.

Sick Kids became our new home. Trisha and I slept beside each other on the three-by-five-foot bench next to Callum's bed. When we weren't in his room or couldn't sleep, we sat in the atrium on the fifth floor looking out the window, crying, praying for strength, and making phone calls to friends and family at all hours of the night. Trisha's parents, called Nana and Papa by our kids, were bringing Thai to us, and my dad, Grandpa Gene, was coming to be with us for as long as we needed him. Our siblings were all making arrangements to come as well. Those days remain a blur. It was the first experience in my life where I felt 100 percent overwhelmed all day long. We were filled with grief, despair, anxiety and fear, and were only keeping ourselves together because we had four little eyes – Callum's and Thai's – looking at us to make everything okay.

Four days after Callum's diagnosis, Dr. Rutka was set to perform the surgery to remove the tumour from the back of his brain. When we arrived at the operating room at 7 a.m., Dr. Rutka, the pre-op nurses, the anaesthetist, and everyone else who was there guided us through what to expect. They were compassionate and demonstrated expertise.

Walking down the hallway to the O.R., I talked to the anaesthetist who would put Callum to sleep and keep him unconscious during the operation. He was about to be given a full anaesthetic and have his skull cut open, and his neurosurgeon would attempt to remove all his tumour. Feeling like I was in the middle of a horrible dream, I said to the anaesthetist, sputtering the words, with tears streaming down my face, "I promise I'll be good." She said, "Stop. Don't say that. No, you won't. You're the dad, so be Callum's dad. Cry, hold his hand, be a disaster. We'll take care of him and we'll take care of you while you're in the operating room. This is about you too, not just him." Wow! That blew my mind. It was the perfect thing for her to say and exactly what I needed. Her confidence, promise, and clear instructions to not be stoic were so powerful in that moment. She gave me the courage to be vulnerable that day and I carried her words with me from then on.

While the team in the O.R. was caring for Callum, we were told we had between six and ten hours to wait before Dr. Rutka finished the surgery, and an indeterminate amount of time before we could see our Callum in the post-op recovery room. We knew the risk of death from surgery was low but not zero. We also knew the intra-operative findings and risks of complications during surgery were significant. Based on the location of the tumour, there were very real chances Callum might not walk or talk properly ever again, or eat independently, or be able to use his hands, or truly be himself. We tried to prepare ourselves for anything.

After a grueling day of waiting, walking, pacing, crying, and praying, Dr. Rutka came to see us in the waiting room. Everything had gone well. He had removed the entire tumour and Callum was just starting to wake up in the recovery room. We could see him shortly. We were told the tumour had an abnormal consistency, that it was more liquid than they had expected. This wasn't either good or bad, just atypical, and he wasn't sure if it had any specific significance. More tests would follow to direct the path of Callum's chemotherapy and/or radiation treatments. We understood we had a very long road ahead of us, but Callum had made it through the first step, and this was worth allowing ourselves to feel tremendous relief.

Moments after our meeting with Dr. Rutka, we were allowed into the recovery room to see our baby. He was tired from a big surgery and a bit uncomfortable. There he was, at two and a half, as perfect as he'd been that morning lying in his pre-op bed. With tears pouring down our faces, I asked Callum the test question I'd prepped him for over the last few days, anticipating this very moment. "Callum, who's Daddy's big boy?" He replied immediately with a smile, "I am, Daddy. I am." In that instant, I knew our boy was there. His personality and ability to communicate were intact. If he never walked again, I didn't care. Our Callum was telling us he was still himself.

Later that night, Trisha and I met the Intensive Care Unit (ICU) physician who was in charge during the initial hours following Callum's surgery. We chatted for a long time and shared our story. He made an impression on us. He was caring, and he spent a long time talking to Trisha about the similarities between his family's life and our life. He had noticed Callum was underweight and wondered whether there was another issue, beyond the brain tumour, that might explain it. Could Callum have a milder form of cystic fibrosis? Could he have a bowel malabsorption problem? We didn't know, and finding answers would have to wait until the chemotherapy was done.

The first week of post-operative recovery was tough for Callum. He was uncomfortable. He had pain. He didn't want to eat and he couldn't get out of bed. To add insult to injury, he had a hard time lifting his legs. That's how weak he was after his brain had literally been pushed around and poked at during surgery. It might take a long time for his muscles to achieve normal movement and coordination. Luckily for Callum, and for Trisha and me, Thai was able to visit often with Trisha's parents in tow, and from his first visit he was comfortable climbing right into bed with Callum. Big brother Thai didn't miss a beat. He adapted the games he wanted to play with his little brother so they could play together. All of a sudden, our boys were side by side and smiling again. We started to develop a daytime routine. Sick Kids truly had become our new home.

Nighttime was a different story. It was far more challenging. The silence, the darkness, and the loneliness were tough on Trisha and me, and Callum wasn't sleeping very well. He had difficulties getting comfortable and then slept in fits and starts, and he was more irritable at night as a result of his surgery and his age. On the second night post-op, since things had settled down a little bit, I went to sleep at a friend's, who lived in an apartment nearby. I got a call from Trisha at about 2 a.m. She was frantic. Something was wrong with Callum. She couldn't describe it, but something was definitely wrong. I hung up the phone, grabbed my things, and rushed out the door. I had to run up University Avenue to reach the hospital, I'm not sure how many blocks, but it seemed like much further than I could bear.

The only way to get into Sick Kids at that hour were the front doors, so that's where I ran, and then up the stairs to the fifth floor as fast as I could. When I arrived, I quickly realized Callum was delirious, a common condition I'd witnessed and learned about during medical school and residency training. It was likely a side effect of his surgery, new medications, poor sleep, and ongoing pain. After speaking with the nurse and resident on-call about how to help him feel more comfortable and get settled, I comforted Trisha and promised her I would stay every night until this phase of recovery was over. I was super thankful I was in medicine during that time. It kept both of us calm.

The month of June continued on and there were many meetings with oncology specialists, social workers, and allied healthcare professionals about the next phase of Callum's treatment. To plan his treatment protocol and start chemotherapy, he needed a definitive diagnosis, which required a tissue sample from his surgery and a spinal fluid sample two weeks post-surgery. He also needed many other investigations and treatments. These included:

- an IV access catheter placed permanently in his chest

- a gastric tube placed permanently in his stomach for nutrition

- the harvesting of his stem cells, which were frozen and stored for future use

- an echocardiogram of his heart

- a follow-up MRI of his brain

- a nuclear medicine scan of his kidneys

- almost daily blood work

- repeated spinal taps

- hearing tests

- a speech and language assessment

Every day seemed to introduce new healthcare providers and a different test, and with it fresh reasons to be worried. During this time, we also moved into a room at Ronald McDonald House (RMH), about a ten-minute walk away. We were promised that the room was ours until the end of Callum's treatment. It was a great relief to have a home outside of the hospital where Thai could sleep with one of us every night. We were welcomed to RMH by the staff and we familiarized ourselves with the shared kitchen and child-life resources.

One afternoon, Trisha and I sat down with the hematology-oncology team to have "the talk." The purpose was to inform us of the final diagnosis of Callum's brain tumour, the prognosis, and the treatment path that lay ahead of us. The news was beyond our worst fears. We were told that Callum had a rare type of tumour that had no known cure. Radiation and chemotherapy, along with surgery, had been used in the past with numerous complications and terrible outcomes.

What we were facing, according to the latest clinical research, was watching Callum undergo a new, experimental protocol that would test the limits of his body again and again, with only a small hope that this time there would be a cure without brain damage. The problem was, as the team clearly articulated, the chemotherapy might kill him. We sat and listened to how toxic it would be, the high risk of complications, which would increase over time, and the very scary road ahead. Up until now, we had been thinking mostly of whether the cancer could come back sometime in the future, but this conversation stopped us in our tracks.

We learned that Callum's treatment would be defined by chemotherapy alone, with no radiation due to the permanent structural brain damage it would cause. Just the chemotherapy would put him at risk of numerous dangerous complications, some of which were unavoidable. Dr. Ute Bartels, who led the meeting and impressed us immediately with her wonderfully caring, compassionate, and honest communication style, told us again and again that Callum's path was different from almost every other child's. His type of cancer, at his age, hadn't previously been cured successfully. In plain words: no child had survived it.

With the experimental protocol, there was, perhaps, a slim chance of cure moving forward, but the journey would be horribly complicated, arduous, and full of peril. Essentially, the best specialists in the world had no choice but to put Callum through six escalating cycles of life-threatening chemotherapy, cycles that would make him incredibly weak and terribly sick. He would also require not one, but three stem cell transplants, one after each of the last three cycles, with the purpose of saving his life. Finally, the protocol demanded that Callum be in strict isolation at Sick Kids for cycles four, five, and six.

Dr. Bartels told us that this type of treatment hadn't been done exactly in this way, for this tumour, for this young and small a child, ever before at Sick Kids or even in Canada. But it was the only chance we had of helping Callum live to his fifth birthday and possibly be cured. No other options provided any hope of him one day being healthy again.

So there it was. We would be forced to watch our Callum suffer tremendous amounts of discomfort, nausea and pain to give him a chance at living. Each month would be harder than the previous one, and each month would mean more danger, pain, and struggle just for Callum to stay alive. We would do all this in an attempt to prevent the cancer from coming back. It was made very clear. There was no other option, no other path to take. This was what we were about to face together.

CHAPTER 3

Summer of Chemotherapy

On the last day of June, Callum was given permission to move back home to receive his first three chemotherapy cycles under the supervision of Dr. Silva at Kingston General. Behind the scenes, she had fought hard to get us transferred for the summer, knowing it would be difficult for us to be at Sick Kids for all six cycles. With courage, we packed up our minivan, left the hospital with a million instructions from a myriad of healthcare providers, and got on the highway. Driving the 401 during the holiday weekend was exhausting. A trip that normally took three hours became six hours stuck in traffic, construction, and slowdowns due to car accidents. It was especially tough to see how uncomfortable Callum was in his car seat, with worsening neck and back pain, his surgery just four weeks behind him. Our only relief was knowing we would soon be home again, sleeping in our own beds.

Callum's first chemotherapy cycle started on July 1, Canada Day, less than twenty-four hours after leaving Sick Kids. We were admitted to the pediatric ward, where we met Dr. Silva. Within two hours of the drugs infusing into Callum's IV line, he started vomiting. Watching our two-year-old retch and retch into a bucket was horrible. We wished we could trade places with him, but that wasn't possible. And so it began. Trisha and I cried continuously – in the hallway, in the bathroom, in the next room – anywhere we could that was away from Callum.

That first night, Trisha stayed in the hospital and I drove home to be with Thai. The plan was for Trisha and me to be at the hospital together during the day, and at night we would alternate going home to be with our older son. During the day, Thai would visit with Callum as much as possible, and we would figure out how other family members could come for visits too. Doctor's orders, hospital visiting rules, and our own need for quiet and sleep made it extra difficult. Callum was weak and vomiting regularly. We struggled to know how to coorindate everything.

Although Thai had never spent an entire night in our bed at home before, the first night I was alone with him I asked if maybe when Callum was in the hospital, he would like to sleep with Mommy or me. Understandably, he was lonely for his brother and having a hard time falling asleep. He said yes, and then we agreed that when Callum was well enough to come home between chemotherapy cycles, he would be okay to sleep in his own bed. After we figured out the routine that first night, Thai fell right asleep.

Now that we were in Kingston again, other matters required attention. The day Callum was admitted to hospital back at the end of May, my work was put on hold for the weekend. Three days later Callum was diagnosed with a brain tumour. Work was placed on hold indefinitely. During that time our family took care of everything. Now we had a six-month treatment path ahead of us and I had to think about my training, work responsibilities, all kinds of bills, grocery shopping, house maintenance, and many other things that needed looking after.

My supervisors at work gave me medical/family leave for six months and said I could let them know how I wanted to move forward from there. As for the house, paying bills was relatively straightforward, as was grocery shopping. Our parents, in particular, were an important part of our financial safety net. They sat us down and mapped out a plan of support that would ensure we could focus on Callum and Thai and not worry about the added costs that were coming our way. Friends and immediate family looked after lawn maintenance and so much else.

Our life became streamlined to accommodate two priorities: to be at the hospital with Callum at all times and to make sure Thai wasn't left behind. The first priority seems obvious, but the second was also critically important to Trisha and me. Thai was our baby too. He needed as much time, attention, love, and joy in his life as any other four-year-old and we were committed to figuring out how we would continue to be the parents we wanted to be for him. He needed Trisha and me to keep our family together no matter how much worry and fear we felt or the long hours we would be spending in Callum's hospital room.

The first weeks of chemotherapy brought with them many changes and challenges. The four of us struggled to find the right routine and family balance amidst the chaos. The onslaught of new healthcare workers in our life was one of the hardest issues to deal with. There were very few hours of the day that weren't interrupted by nurses, physicians, social workers, dieticians, or coordinators. All these people were needed to provide care for Callum and they wanted to be available, but their presence wasn't critical each and every time they came into his room. We noticed the lack of coordinated meetings, which would have allowed those who were more peripherally involved to update us on what was happening on a less frequent basis.

I remember sometimes being unsympathetic with members of the healthcare team. People would say, "I'm here for you, whatever you need, just let me know." But to this day, I'm not convinced everyone meant it. This may seem harsh, but it's true. When Trisha and I asked for the smallest bit of privacy, or for coordinated care that would give some sense of daily routine, or for less frequent non-essential interruptions, all of which we thought were possible, we were rarely successful. It was very frustrating to try to set limits on communication that wasn't absolutely necessary. What amounted to a brief "pop in" disturbed Callum's sleep, interrupted short visits with family or rare moments when Trisha and I were alone with each other, and destroyed any sense of quiet, peacefulness, or reflection.

Mostly our response was, "Thank you for letting us know you're available. We appreciate the role you're playing in Callum's care and we'll get a hold of you when we need you. We're okay for now. Thanks so much." We did ask for help when we needed it, but we tried to balance this with asking for privacy when possible. Callum required a high level of daily care that involved various IV medications and fluids, blood products, medical assessments, and monitoring his vital signs, so opportunities for privacy were minimal during daytime hours. This reality, we learned, was an unexpected but very common challenge when your child is admitted to hospital with a critical illness. Your child's room becomes your home, but you have little or no control over almost everything that enters it. Everyone was trying to help, but sometimes as a result of efforts that were needlessly intrusive, interactions were strained, causing us more stress and less time with Callum.

With so many medications, infusions, and interventions required, mistakes weren't uncommon.This could be a medication given at the wrong time, the omission of a medication, or the wrong medication given. It could be no flow in Callum's central intravenous line, a wrong and sometimes dangerous decision made by the resident physician on-call, or an IV port becoming contaminated or blocked, or a combination of any of these. Most issues were small and we understood that mistakes happen, but some were more worrisome and put Callum's welfare at risk. Often a collection of small mistakes led to a bigger mistake or an action taken that had frightening consequences.

During one particular incident, when a senior resident gave a medical student the task of unblocking Callum's central line, Trisha called me at home to say she felt very uneasy. After listening to her panic about the safety of Callum's central venous catheter, I coached her to tell the medical student to stop what she was doing and seek help before making a mistake. I told her that Dr. Silva could be paged at any time if a proper and safe solution wasn't found.

The next day we asked for a team meeting to review what had happened and to discuss a number of smaller incidents we'd experienced in the previous weeks, like communication issues, no-flow states in Callum's central line for more than 15 minutes, and other safety concerns. We were thankful Dr. Silva listened carefully, asked for points of clarification, then promised she would examine the system issues we had raised. She assured us that it was her job to be our biggest advocate and that we shouldn't shy away from making requests or giving feedback at any time. She said that it was our responsibility to help identify patient safety concerns so she could figure out how to make meaningful change, if needed, over the things she could control.

One of the unique challenges I struggled with during this time was being a physician in the hospital where Callum was a patient. Interacting with the ER and the pediatric nursing staff and medical colleagues I had worked with and come to know was a tough dynamic to navigate. I wondered how to be the best parent advocate I could be for Callum while maintaining my professionalism. Early on, I discovered the tension between these two opposing realities. At times it was impossible to be both an understanding colleague and a strong voice for my family.

This created a lot of conflict in my mind. The needs of Callum, Trisha, and Thai demanded that I protect them without regard for the feelings of the medical team. But being a physician demanded that I interact with the nursing staff and my medical colleagues with a high level of professionalism that precluded me from speaking up when I was unhappy, dissatisfied, or, frankly, ticked off. It wasn't lost on me that no matter what happened, one day I would be working as a physician in that hospital again. Asking for a team meeting had been a big decision. I knew that my single most important role was being Callum's advocate.

There were also advantages to being a physician-parent at the hospital where I worked. One special moment that arose from this dynamic involved overseeing a first-year pediatric resident, named Ziad, perform a physical exam on Callum. Acting as a medical teacher and helping train younger doctors was a regular part of my job as a senior ER resident, but to do so when the patient was my two-and-a-half-year-old son was unique. It was fun to help Ziad (affectionately known as Z) through his fear of examining a very sick patient in front of me, a senior resident ER physician and also the dad. I can only imagine how intimidated I would have been in his position. Jumping back and forth between the roles of dad, supervising physician, and teacher, I helped Callum and Z establish a relationship that allowed Z to do his job, overcome his fear, and feel confident that he was a valued member of the pediatric team. Unbeknownst to us at the time, this moment we shared was the beginning of a bond that would continue in the years ahead.

Other challenges unrelated to the chemotherapy and medical care surfaced as well. Specifically, interactions with family members were tough at times. Callum wasn't allowed many visitors, and when he was, he was very tired and increasingly looked unwell. This was distressing for family to see and deal with. Grandparents who are wonderful at providing love and support can easily become overwhelmed and incapacitated with grief. The few times they were allowed to visit Callum in hospital were crushing. He was terribly sick and there was no pretending otherwise.

This was especially true for Trisha's parents, Nana and Papa, who were used to seeing and playing with Callum on a weekly basis. Now he was mostly confined to his bed with extreme fatigue and nausea, and with multiple IV infusions running at once. Nana's bag of tricks, which usually made our kids laugh and feel loved, was no match for Callum's critical illness. Too much laughing or carrying on, even from his bed, would make him vomit almost instantly.

My parents were uncertain about how best to support Trisha and me. My dad, also an ER doctor, stayed largely in the background, dropping in and out of the ward, waiting for our instructions, trying to think of ways to help. Just being around so we could have a shower in the morning, or bringing us coffee or offering to do groceries, were small things that all added up. My mom, known as Granny by our boys, generally stayed at home and supported us from afar. She was always available by phone to listen when I needed to talk. In my mind, she was "on call" for anything.

Often, what I needed most was to cry with her and let her tell me it was okay to be afraid of what might come. She helped in her short spurts of consoling me on the phone, and her advice was also welcome. This included reminders to let myself be scared or sad, to stay firm in being Callum's strongest advocate, to be a good parent to Thai, and to hold Trisha's hand, literally and figuratively, throughout our struggle. My mom, more than anyone else, reinforced the idea that Trisha and I didn't need to apologize for knowing what was best for us, and that we would find our way forward if we looked after each other. This proved over time to be the best advice.

In the hospital, there were many happy and bittersweet moments too. One of them was when Callum had his hair cut by the hospital hairdresser after his first round of chemotherapy. I vividly remember, during one of Thai's visits, hearing the two boys discuss how great this new "bald head" haircut was. Callum said, "Look, Thai, I got a haircut. Do you like it?" Thai replied, "It looks great. I really like it." When he went over to rub Callum's head, he gave his little brother a big smile to confirm he really did think it was great.

Other special moments included re-enacting TV episodes from the children's cartoon Max & Ruby. This was Callum's favourite show, maybe because the lead character, a preschool bunny named Max who was always causing trouble for his older sister Ruby, was as precocious and mischievous as Callum. One evening, we used my cellphone to call the phone in the hospital room to act out an episode called "Louise's Secret" in which Max continues to interrupt Ruby's phone conversation. Ruby's friend Louise had called to tell Ruby a secret and Max kept getting in the way. We laughed and laughed so hard. Callum was happy and impressed that Daddy had memorized nearly the entire episode.

Another special memory was the time I went on a hunt for fish crackers. Callum had a very poor appetite due to chemo-induced nausea and getting calories into him had become an ever-increasing struggle. One evening we realized he had run out of his favourite fish crackers. Off I went to the grocery store before it closed. On my arrival, I was amazed to find not two or three kinds of fish crackers, but at least a dozen. There were orange ones, yellow ones, rainbow-coloured ones, big ones, small ones, and more. Wow! How could I decide? This was before texting, which meant I had to make an executive decision right there and then. I think I spent $40 on fish crackers that night. I bought every kind. Who knew splurging on fish crackers could cause so much joy. When I returned to the hospital, Callum was excited to line them all up, and he had a ball organizing which ones he'd eat and in what order.

Trisha similarly created many special moments with Callum. She taught him the alphabet and put alphabet posters up on the wall, and she taught him the number scale. She read him lots of books, seemingly non-stop for weeks and months. She played I Spy with him and brought toys from home to play with on the bed, and when Callum had a room overlooking Lake Ontario, the two of them eagerly watched as ORNGE emergency helicopters transported patients to and from the helipad across the street. This was very exciting, especially at nighttime, when you could hear the bright orange helicopter approaching from far away.

More than anything else, Trisha fostered an attitude that home was wherever Callum was. Every time we had a new hospital room, it would be transformed into Callum's room, like he had at home. The difference was, everything was sterilized with hand sanitizer, so as not to bring germs into his environment. Tupperware containers full of toys were organized and stacked neatly in the corner, snacks were arranged on the windowsill, the computer was set up for Sesame Street, Internet surfing, and watching movies, and puzzles and books were placed within easy reach. Even Callum's favourite posters decorated the walls.

He particularly liked the alphabet poster and enjoyed playing "the name game" with Mommy, where he would think of someone's name for each letter of the alphabet. We loved listening to him identify letters for family members and for the doctors and nurses who cared for him. Dr. Silva and Uncle Vico were his favourites for S and V. On my drive home to Thai at night, I often thought that Trisha and I could make Callum happy no matter how unwell he felt, as long as we were together.

There were also many scary moments during the two months we were in Kingston. Callum's first three cycles brought with them many complications besides the challenges of living ninety percent of our life in a hospital. We endured his central line clotting repeatedly, numerous medication errors, dangerously low blood counts, pneumonia, a pulmonary hemorrhage, gastric tube infections, nutrition errors, and poor communication between the team members. The mistakes were big and small, and could be attributed to every level of care provider, including Trisha and me. Most importantly, though, they were the consequences of Callum's critical illness, having been induced by the aggressive chemotherapy protocol. The arduous path Dr. Bartels at Sick Kids had described to us before starting chemotherapy had become a painful, sobering, and frightening reality.

Non-stop nausea and vomiting, abdominal pain, terrible fatigue, the pulmonary hemorrhage, and an episode of febrile neutropenia[1] after each chemotherapy cycle required immediate ER visits, followed by readmission to hospital, multiple tests to search for a possible source of infection, and broad-spectrum IV antibiotics. With each cycle and its resulting complications, Callum got sicker. Every episode was terrifying for us as parents. I was particularly distraught about the time that elapsed between Callum having a fever (we already knew his blood counts were dangerously low) and receiving life-saving doses of IV antibiotics.

---

[1] *When a cancer patient's body has a vulnerable immune system, febrile neutropenia signifies that a life-threatening infection is likely occurring. Any infection, even the common cold, can kill.*

As a physician, I struggled to shut out the mental imagery of Callum's body having no immune system to fight off invading organisms that could overwhelm his organs and claim his life. I remember on one occasion waiting in the ER isolation room for an experienced nurse to access the central line IV port in his chest. Apparently, no one felt comfortable approaching the IV port of Dr. Dagnone's critically ill son. After an hour of agony, a nurse not assigned to Callum's care finally arrived to perform the necessary steps. By then I was at my wits' end and ready to scream. I felt scared, trapped, and powerless to help my own son, and even though I was an ER physician in my own ER, I was barely holding it together.

Getting through those episodes of febrile neutropenia wasn't any easier because I was a doctor. It probably made it much worse. The knowledge I had made me more scared because I understood the severe consequences of making a mistake in treatment. On the three occasions Callum had febrile neutropenia, the diagnoses entertained included simple scalp infections (cellulitis/impetigo), pneumonia, pulmonary bleeding (hemorrhage), and necrotizing fasciitis (a life-threatening skin infection). The day the pediatric general surgeon was concerned Callum might have necrotizing fasciitis of his abdominal wall was the worst day imaginable. These infections kill healthy young people with immune systems functioning at 100 percent. How would Callum survive with severely compromised defences? He couldn't possibly. I cried and prayed and cried during the whole forty-eight-hour stretch when it was being considered. Thankfully, the cause of his infection proved to be something else.

Over time, our routine at Kingston General consisted of chemotherapy for a week in hospital, then home for two or three days if we were lucky, then to the clinic for an appointment that lasted between four and eight hours, then all of a sudden back to the ER with fever, then readmitted to the ward for a few days, then on to the next round of chemotherapy. This was the pattern for the first three cycles, with each cycle taking more out of Callum. His nausea, vomiting, and profound fatigue grew worse. The colour of his skin alone was alarming. As it turned greyer and greyer, we became more fearful that we might not escape the chemotherapy treatment intact. It had become quite clear that we were far more afraid of the treatment than the risk of Callum's cancer returning in the future.

Being able to go home together for a few days after each cycle was always exciting because the four of us could be together all day long. We could also have family over to visit in the comfort of our home. During our time at Kingston General, Callum was at home for a total of only eight days out of sixty over July and August. And on three of them we had to be at the cancer clinic for part or all of the day for medical assessments, blood work, and IV transfusions. So time at home was sacred. We were always grateful that Dr. Silva had made those days possible so we could laugh, cuddle, cry, and be with each other without everyone on top of us.

Those were for sure the most bittersweet times we spent together. Being home and watching the kids play together was magical. Watching them sit side by side on the couch in front of the TV, fall asleep on each other, giggle and be silly together, brought Trisha and me so much joy. Thai especially was incredibly good to Callum. At only four years old, he understood that Callum was sick and couldn't play for very long. When Callum got tired, he would lie down on the floor or on the couch and Thai would follow his lead. Thai would end up lying right beside him and they would continue their pretend game or watching a TV show without missing a beat. For Thai, doing anything with his little brother was better than being without him.

Thai was also Callum's de facto physiotherapist. After his surgery, Callum had to learn to walk again. Thai led him through it. After each round of chemotherapy, Callum would come home so exhausted, weak, and deconditioned that he could barely stand up. Within one afternoon of playing with his brother, Callum would somehow find the energy to first walk around the ottoman, then progress to walking to the toy shelves some twenty feet away so he could play with Thai as he always did. After the third cycle, Callum asked if his cousins Claire, Jacob, and Turner could come over to play and have popsicles. Callum was never so proud as when he showed his cousins how he could walk all the way down the driveway and back up again. Although he didn't have the energy to walk for longer than a few minutes, the pictures we took of the five of them licking their popsicles remains to this day one of my all-time favourite memories of our boys and their cousins.

Other special moments during this brief time included watching the boys create a new game called Puppet Theatre. During Puppet Theatre, the four of us would re-enact our favourite stories on the rug floor in the basement. We played out our performances with stick puppets and a miniature fabric stage we put on the coffee table. I was particularly gifted at playing the Big Bad Wolf in The Three Little Pigs. I would call the pigs with a sweet, quiet voice – "Little pigs, little pigs, let me come in…" followed by a more demanding, deeper, louder voice – "Then I'll huff and I'll puff…" with lots of exaggerated huffing and puffing. The boys loved when I blew big gusts of air in their faces as I was blowing the houses down. They laughed the hardest when I pretended to pass out from not being able to blow the brick house down at the end. We played this endlessly, never tiring of the story.

Trisha's favourite story came from the book Cook-a Doodle-Doo about a bunch of farm animals trying to make strawberry shortcake. She had always been a busy baker at our house so this story was especially fitting for her. We had puppets of all the characters and the whole thing was very silly. I enjoyed sitting back and watching Trisha entertain Thai and Callum with her performances, much as she must have enjoyed my Big Bad Wolf entreaties to the pigs. These were the moments we most loved.

After just a few days at home we would always end up back at the hospital. Callum's blood counts were very low and he easily developed a fever, which meant automatic readmission to the hospital and IV antibiotics and transfusions. Following the third chemotherapy cycle we got only two whole days at home. One afternoon while Callum, the pediatric nurse, and I were watching his blood transfusion finish, Dr. Silva told me I could take Callum outside for some fresh air. No more than an hour, she said, maybe two, as long as I was careful. So off we went, with Callum sitting in the wagon with a hat to protect him from the sun and a blanket to keep him warm.

It was a beautiful afternoon and we found ourselves in the park across the street wandering the pathways and looking at the birds and flowers and the kids playing on the climber in the distance. We talked about how it was hard not to run around and have fun, and Callum said, "Daddy, when the medicine makes me better, can I play on the climber again?" "Yes honey, of course," I said with tears in my eyes. We continued to wander, bumped into a few friends and visited briefly, then settled in the shade under a large maple tree. Callum was tired and lay back on the pillow in the wagon. I tucked the blanket around him and stroked his bald head as he fell asleep. This seemed to be the perfect place to take a nap, and was definitely a better spot to spend the afternoon than in the hospital.

After sitting for a few minutes, I decided to lie down on the grass. I cried on and off for the next hour. I was afraid this might be the last time we would be together like this in a park. I was afraid of having to return to Sick Kids in just another week or two for more dangerous chemotherapy and stem cell transplants. I was afraid I couldn't protect him. I was afraid for Trisha and me having to live in the world without him. Tears poured down my face and every few minutes I'd pull myself together as people walked past us.

After almost two hours it was time to go back to the hospital. But rather than go straight back, we took a small detour to get a banana popsicle, which everybody knew was Daddy's favourite. It made me so happy to watch Callum lick his half of the popsicle and see it dripping down his chin. We agreed that banana was definitely the best flavour for a popsicle ever. We walked for a few minutes, oblivious to the fact that Callum was ill and undergoing chemotherapy. At the end of our awalk, just before arriving at the hospital, we came to the top of the hill at Arch Street. I had walked up and down this little hill many times as a student and medical resident but never really appreciated its moderate incline.

Taking advantage of the opportunity that appeared before us, Callum and I left the sidewalk and went to the middle of the street. There were no parked cars on the road and no cars were coming towards us. It was a one-way street. Everything looked safe. I asked Callum if he wanted to ride down the hill with Daddy and of course the answer was a big "Yes!" After checking one last time for cars, I climbed into the wagon behind Callum and folded the handle back so we could steer.

I gave a gentle push with my feet and we were off. I kept my legs hanging over the sides until I knew we were in the clear, then down we went. For ten seconds we cruised down that hill in the middle of the street with the wind flying through our hair and Callum giggling with delight. When the wagon came to a stop at the bottom we gave each other high fives and promised not to tell Mommy or Dr. Silva for a long time, knowing we might get in trouble. It was as close to pure joy as I'd ever felt in my entire life. Minutes later we were back in Callum's room preparing for another blood transfusion and accepting that our afternoon of freedom had come to an end.

A few days later the end of August was upon us and Callum had finished his first three cycles of chemotherapy. It was time to get ready to return to Toronto for cycles four, five, and six. We'd been told these next three cycles would make the first three seem easy to manage in comparison. That was a very scary thought after what we'd been through already. By videoconference earlier in August, the transplant specialist at Sick Kids had warned us about the extreme isolation Callum would be subjected to for three months, the new dangers we would face with the three stem cell-transplant rescue procedures, and the significant risk of chemotherapy-induced leukemia, lymphoma, and early-onset osteoporosis, and an immune-compromised state that Callum would live with for the rest of his life. After all we'd been through in the past three months, we were quite afraid of what was yet to come.

CHAPTER 4

A Long Way to Go

Getting ready to leave was overwhelming. Callum was still on the pediatric ward at Kingston General but in a few days he would be settled in at Sick Kids. There were so many unknowns and things beyond our control that lay ahead. We'd been through so much already, yet we needed to prepare ourselves and our children for more to come. We had a lot to do in a very short time. Trisha and I weren't sure how to plan but we did our best.

Part of preparing for the isolation of Callum's upcoming chemotherapy and stem cell transplants was allowing everyone in our family to see him before we left. Trisha and I decided that a great way to achieve this would be to throw Callum an early third birthday party on Labour Day weekend. The location would be City Park beside the hospital. His actual birthday wasn't for another eight weeks, but we knew this might be our only chance to have a real party for him.

We would have cake, balloons, jello, chips, Kentucky Fried Chicken, grandparents, cousins, aunts, uncles, and everything else you'd expect for a child's birthday party. The only problem was that Callum was very sick. His blood counts were terribly low (Hgb 56, Plts 22, WBC 2.6) and his energy was almost non-existent. He shouldn't have been getting out of bed, let alone going to the park for a party. But this was our only chance before we'd be gone for at least three months. Thankfully, Dr. Silva understood the importance of the occasion and granted us a small window of time away from the hospital.

I vividly remember the walk to the park, pulling Callum in the wagon with one hand and holding Trisha's hand with the other. Our family was in the distance with the balloons and cake. Everyone was there. As we got closer, an ominous feeling came over me and I became increasingly scared. Callum had a dangerous path ahead of him and I knew there was a very real possibility this could be the last time we were all together.

But the party was a smashing success. We had so much fun. Everyone was really excited to see Callum, and he was equally excited to see all his cousins, aunts, uncles, and grandparents. Somewhere in his little body, despite his illness, he found the smiles and happy spirit we'd all come to know since he was an infant. He enjoyed his orange jello snacks, the balloons, his cake, and everything else we'd prepared for him. Thai, likewise, was having the best time he'd had since Disney World. He enjoyed the company of his extended family and was thrilled to play with his cousins.

Luckily for us it was a beautiful sunny day and the kids had a blast playing football, frisbee, and soccer. Then, all of a sudden, there was Callum on his feet. Not to be left behind, he was running with his cousins as best he could, then kicking the soccer ball. How he managed to stand, let alone run and play, even for a few brief minutes, was astounding. He hadn't run since before his surgery three months earlier and really had barely walked in that time. After five minutes of activity, the reality of his illness overtook his excitement. He had to stop and lie down on my shoulder. It was time to go back to the hospital. We took a few family pictures and then back we went. I can't remember how long we were at the park. Maybe an hour? It's all a blur. It was magical and bittersweet and devastating. Callum fell asleep in the wagon during the five-minute walk to his room.

The next two days saw Trisha and me packing for the move to Toronto. Our room at Ronald McDonald House was waiting for us and Callum would have a new room on the hematology-oncology ward on the eighth floor of Sick Kids. We struggled to figure out exactly what we would need for the next three months, so in the end we packed everything. I figured that since we had a minivan, we could bring anything we wanted to. We packed bicycles, a running stroller, clothes, books, puzzles, food, and many other things. Thai and I had fun filling suitcases with toys for him and Callum. We stuffed them with train sets, toy cars, and whatever else we could jam in there. Rules didn't apply except for one – if it fit in the van, it could come.

Our friends Terry and Carolyn, who had known us for twenty years, gave us the best going away gift ever – a huge gift certificate from our favourite toy store in town to buy anything the boys wanted. Telling them about it and watching their excitement was a great moment in itself. After much deliberation and strategic planning, Thai and Callum made their choices. Thai decided on a Thomas the Train roundhouse for all his toy trains and Callum chose a puppy kennel for his beloved stuffed puppy, which he'd slept with since he was born. The visit to the store fuelled the kids with enough excitement to get them to Toronto without any anxiety or tears.

Following close behind us on our journey back to Toronto was my dad. Grandpa Gene helped with the move into RMH, then he stayed with Thai so Trisha and I could "go out on the town" with Callum for an hour or two before bedtime. He was to be readmitted to Sick Kids the next day. With Callum riding in his stroller, we watched the streetcars, walked along University Avenue, and stopped for a snack beside the hospital. Callum and I split a decadent double chocolate chip brownie. It was surreal. In the next twenty-four hours our life would once again be dictated by tests and chemotherapy, but at that moment we had all the freedom in the world.

The three of us walked back to RMH. Callum climbed into bed with Thai to sleep with him one last time. Tomorrow everything would be different. The boys would be isolated from each other for the next three months. They wouldn't be allowed to be in the same room together, let alone touch each other. We said goodnight to my dad and thanked him for helping us enjoy those few precious hours. Tomorrow would be a big day for all of us.

The next morning, Callum was admitted to the hematology-oncology ward as planned. We met a few new doctors, many new nurses, and were prepped on the various protocols for medications, tests, and strict isolation procedures. The protocol for chemotherapy cycles four, five, and six included many new rules. Except for Trisha and me, Callum couldn't have visitors during the first three weeks of each cycle. For two of those weeks, he wouldn't be allowed to leave his room because of his immuno-compromised status. His blood counts would be so low that any minor infection could kill him. As a result, he was scheduled for three stem cell transplants, one at the end of each cycle. The stem cells in his bone marrow that had been wiped out by the chemotherapy would be replaced with his own healthy, blood-forming stem cells, which had previously been collected, processed, frozen, and stored in the laboratory.

For the coming months, Trisha and I would be prohibited from touching Callum unless absolutely necessary. How we would care for our critically ill child who was isolated from the world without holding him was too impossible and frightening to contemplate. But we had no choice. This protocol was the only chance Callum had. So Trisha and I both took a big breath and promised each other we'd get through it together. I told myself that I would do whatever Callum, Thai, and Trisha needed of me. I was a dad first, a husband second, and an individual a distant third. This was no time to worry about me. Anyway, Trisha had worrying about me covered. In her mind, I knew that Trisha was a mom first, a wife second, and an individual a very distant third. We would take responsibility for looking after each other. We didn't say this out loud. We didn't have to. It was a simple truth that made the most sense to us, and it carried us forward.

Adapting to our new reality was challenging. Thai and Callum were separated, which meant Trisha and I were separated too. Like the last three months, we alternated responsibilities and the time we spent with each of our kids. But this was different. We were in Toronto without our extended family. We had to figure out how it was going to work. A few key decisions needed to be made, and the first one involved Thai. Rather than put him in childcare for part of the day, we decided to start him in junior kindergarten at a great school a few blocks away from the hospital. Every day, he would have three hours of activities, learning, and opportunities for his own growth. We had toyed with the idea of having him stay in Kingston with family so he could start kindergarten with his friends, but we couldn't imagine being in Toronto without him. Our family home was wherever Callum needed to be.

We sent an inquiry by email to the principal of Orde Street Public School, and were thrilled when he let us know he'd be happy to let Thai enroll in a JK class whenever we were ready. A few days after Callum was readmitted, Thai and I went to check out the school and chat with the principal in person. Barely keeping it together, I explained our situation and said that Trisha and I needed a safe, nurturing place for Thai to learn and grow. Just as I hoped, he looked me in the eye and said, "I'll do whatever I can for you and your family. We'd love to have Thai in JK here." Then he asked if I wanted him to start that day.

A few minutes later, the principal lifted Thai off my lap. As he carried him to his new classroom, he assured me that my son would be okay, even if he had to clear his schedule that morning to stay with Thai to make sure he got settled in. I knew this was the right move, but it was so hard, and I was glad it was me there and not Mommy. In that moment, I was eternally grateful to the principal and Orde Street Public School for embracing us.

Back at the hospital, Callum had undergone many tests and assessments with specialists. Then his fourth cycle of chemotherapy started. As expected, he was immediately nauseated and vomited frequently. During that period, many nurses commented that they had never seen a child vomit so frequently from chemotherapy. Was this because his chemotherapy was more toxic? Was there something else wrong? Or was Callum just easily nauseated? We didn't know. No matter what the reason, Trisha and I were helpless to make it better.

The new isolation protocol made everything so much harder. Though we'd known it was coming, there was no way to fully prepare. We had toys, puzzles, books, a computer, stickers, movies, and each other, but we were trapped in a ten-by-fourteen-foot room and that made all the difference. In 2006, there was no Skype, no Facetime, and no way to text pictures from a phone. We didn't even own a cellphone until the day after Callum was diagnosed. Owning two seemed crazy as phone plans were prohibitively expensive at that time. In any event, there was a hiccup. Although Apple had developed a preliminary application for videoconferencing by cellphone, the Sick Kids dial-up connection didn't support the program because the application was too advanced for their system.

For communicating with the outside world we had email and a land line in Callum's room. Both had their limitations. Talking on the phone meant Callum would overhear us, which bothered us, and anyway, if we were in the room, we wanted to give all our attention to him. Also, it was emotional and exhausting to talk on the phone to anyone other than Trisha. Email worked well for group updates, but responding to individuals one at a time was time-consuming, repetitive, and just as emotional and exhausting. To support us, the hematology-oncology service gave us a set of videophones to make calls to Thai at RMH. We were hopeful this would help. Unfortunately, the few calls we made only worsened Callum's spirits. He got so sad and upset when he saw the room at RMH and remembered how much fun he'd had sleeping with Thai our first night back in Toronto. Callum longed to see his brother, to play with him, touch him, laugh with him, and hug him. The videophone had none of those capabilities, so we stopped using it. I wonder now if Skype or Facetime or texting pictures would have made things any better. I'm not so sure.

Another challenge we didn't anticipate was that Callum couldn't have Puppy with him on his bed. In fact, the medical team didn't want Puppy in his room at all because stuffed animals carried dust mites, germs, and dander. Initially, we weren't sure what to do. Puppy had slept with Callum every night since we came home with him from the hospital as a newborn. How do you suddenly separate a child from their blanket or soother or favourite stuffed animal? In the end, we didn't have to take Puppy away. We thought of a clever solution. It was decided that Puppy would undergo his own isolation protocol, which meant staying in his toy kennel on the bedside table. This involved putting him in the dryer for a long time, placing him in a sterile ziplock bag, then sitting him up in the kennel, which first had to be sterilized with an alcohol solution. It was perfect. Puppy would be close by, undergoing the same treatment as Callum. Though he wouldn't be able to touch Puppy, he could see him all day long. To our almost three-year-old, this made a lot of sense.

Other unanticipated challenges quickly became apparent. One was that Callum had to wear pull-ups again. Having graduated to big-boy underwear shortly before his diagnosis, this was a crushing reality for him. But there was no way to manage toileting without reintroducing diapers. Together, Trisha and I explained why being sick, having to stay in bed, and receiving so much medicine meant that he needed to wear pull-ups. We were upset by how unfair it was to take away that developmental milestone from Callum, which he'd been extremely proud of achieving.

Over time, he accepted this reality. We agreed that the train pull-ups were the only ones he wanted to wear. This seemed very reasonable, except when the Shoppers Drug Mart in the hospital was sold out of them. When this happened, I would buy the variety pack despite the fact that only a quarter of the pull-ups were the desired train ones. I didn't care about discarding the remaining three-quarters of the bag, though sometimes at night, when he was too tired to see me tricking him, I used pull-ups with different designs. All this was a very small price to pay for his happiness.

Slowly but surely, we developed a family routine both at RMH and with Callum at the hospital. He was in bed in his room with either Trisha or me at his side 24/7, and Thai went to school every weekday morning and otherwise played at RMH or visited us at the hospital. Our daily schedule adhered to a few key priorities: Thai's school schedule, mealtimes, bedtime, and maximizing opportunities to be together. A typical weekday would unfold in a sequence of predetermined events with Trisha and me switching places and roles on alternate days so that equal time was spent with Callum and Thai. A normal day looked like this...

Daddy and Thai woke up at RMH at 7:30 a.m., showered, got dressed, had breakfast in our room, and left for school at 8:30. On sunny days, Thai rode his bike, complete with training wheels, the ten blocks to school through downtown Toronto. His route followed Gerrard Street to University Avenue, up University past Sick Kids and Toronto General Hospital, then left onto Orde Street. The school was beside Princess Margaret Hospital. On rainy days, we walked up to College Street with all the rush hour commuters to catch the streetcar in front of the old Maple Leaf Gardens. We rode one stop and got off in front of his school, where we locked his little bike to the fence. Thai then ran into the playground to play with his new friends. Often I checked in with his teacher to see how he was doing in class and updated him on how Trisha, Callum, and I were managing at the hospital.

At the same time, Trisha and Callum were waking up at the hospital. When breakfast arrived, Trisha probably ate most of it, since Callum's appetite was so poor. By then, his infusions of medications and chemotherapy had already begun. Before long, the nurse for the day came into the room and introduced herself, and once in a while the physicians from the stem cell-transplant service stood in the hallway to discuss Callum's progress. This was one part of the daily routine that really confused us. The team's interactions with us, or lack thereof, seemed out of place. At times it felt like they were carrying on a secret discussion. Didn't we deserve to be included?

One day I felt compelled to butt in to see what they were discussing. By that time I was wondering if this was a group of uncaring doctors. It seemed a harsh thing to think and I didn't express my frustration out loud. I knew they were very much invested in Callum's care. But why did they keep themselves completely separate from us out there in the hallway? They very rarely looked into the room to acknowledge Trisha or me, nor did they ever invite us to join them. It seemed they existed in their own world, a group of specialist professionals "out there." Our exclusion from their discussions about our son's care and progress was palpable. Trisha and I respected the strict isolation precautions demanded by Callum's regimen, but were confused by the many nurses entering and exiting the room while we weren't invited to talk in the hallway.

If only they could see how secluded we were in this small room with its one bench/bed, one chair, one table, and one window. For weeks at a time our entire day passed in this room, always with the door closed, and we did our best to cope. But it was very lonely, both mentally and emotionally. In the end, there was something lost in the transplant team not learning about us as people and parents, and learning nothing about our boy except his chemotherapy regimen, medical reports, blood work results, and vital signs. The doctors in the hall acted more like highly educated transplant scientists than physicians who cared for people. As a physician myself, I knew the difference. We wished we had more integrated interactions and wondered if all the families with children undergoing this type of chemotherapy and isolation felt as cut off from the transplant team as we did. I was pleased to find out later that since our time at Sick Kids, family-centred care rounds have become standard practice.

To get back to our normal day… After dropping Thai off at school, I walked the few short blocks to the hospital and rode the elevator up to Callum's room. Since no contact was allowed due to the risk of infection, I blew him a big kiss good morning and then kissed Trisha. I sent her to get coffee and, if she hadn't eaten Callum's breakfast, something to eat. I then got caught up with Callum while Mommy was gone. It always seemed like an eternity being away from him overnight, and seeing him again each morning was magical.

Trisha would never be gone for more than a few minutes. When she returned, we spent an hour or so together, just the three of us, though Callum's nurse would need to come in and out of the room many times. At 10 a.m., Trisha left the hospital and went to the YMCA at the corner of Yonge and Leslie for a shower and thirty minutes of exercise. Whether it was a walk on the track, a swim in the pool, or something else, we both needed exercise to help with all the stress we were under. Our social worker, David, had organized our memberships. The YMCA was a blessing as it helped us return to the hospital a little more put together.

When her exercise was done, Trisha walked the ten minutes across Queen's Park to Thai's school to pick him up. He was always excited to talk about his morning and his new friends, who came from Kenya, Thailand, Yugoslavia, and many other countries from around the world. Then they walked and biked down University to Sick Kids to meet Callum and me on the ward. I never got tired of watching Thai ride his bike through the front doors of the hospital, onto the elevator, then down the hallway all the way to Callum's door. After knocking, he waved at Callum to say hi.

For weeks at a time, this was the only interaction between our two boys. How they continued to smile and talk about how much they loved and missed each other amazed Trisha and me and made us very proud. Very seldom did they have tears. Although they were only two and four years old, they were happy and hopeful and understood what Mommy and Daddy told them when we said, "Callum needs special medicine to get better. It will make his body sick before it can make him better." Callum repeated this mantra many times over the course of his treatment. "I'm going to get sick before I get better, right Daddy?"

While Trisha was at the Y, Callum and I had a few hours alone. Most of the time, he was confined to his bed for his chemotherapy and various infusions. Some hours were riddled with horrible nausea and others weren't. We made the best of it. We developed a routine of fun and games and napping when needed. We read books, sang songs, watched his favourite TV shows like Max & Ruby and Dora the Explorer, and chatted about what Thai and Mommy might be doing at that very moment. When we were really lucky, we had letters to open, which often came with special stickers and pictures. They were always beautiful. We were so blessed to have the tremendous support of friends and family who sent us mail and constant well wishes.

One of the games I most enjoyed playing with Callum was Hide-and-Seek. This might seem silly when Callum wasn't able to get out of bed, but we made it work. When it was my turn to hide, I could be anywhere – under the covers, behind the bathroom door, behind the IV pole, under the bed, or on the bench under a blanket with my feet sticking out. We laughed and giggled a lot. When it was my turn to seek and his turn to hide, I never got tired of jumping around the room looking for him in all of Daddy's best hiding spots. He would say, "Daddy, I'm over here under my blanket" or "Daddy, I'm under my pillow." Sometimes Callum would just close his eyes and I'd pretend not to see him until he gave me a hint with his voice. One day, Nurse L, my favourite nurse at Sick Kids, popped in to change the medications on the infusion pump and she found us in the middle of Hide-and-Seek. Without missing a beat, we kept on playing and asked if she wanted to join in. She smiled. I think it was the first time she'd seen this game played under these circumstances. She might also have thought I was a bit nuts.

After having lunch with Trisha outside Callum's room, Thai and I left the hospital for the afternoon while Mommy spent it with Callum. Their routine consisted of reading books seemingly forever, doing puzzles, watching movies on the computer or TV, reading more books and sometimes letters, singing songs, playing with stickers, and looking out the window at the elevator and all the people riding up and down. When Callum napped, Trisha was able to send emails, read, or just be alone to cry without Callum watching.

Thai and I often played outside during our afternoons together. The Ronald McDonald House where we stayed has since moved, but at that time it was across the street from a large courtyard that's part of Ryerson Campus. We went there to throw a ball or hang out or Thai would ride his bike. If the day was rainy we went to the mall to wander around, or we'd make a trip to the dollar store to pick up new toys for Thai and Callum to play with. Callum loved surprises, and as time marched on I did my best to bring something new to his room every day, even if it was worth only a few dollars. This was one of the tricks we learned to cope with his isolation. Surprises and other small gestures went a long way to keeping Callum and Thai happy.

Bringing toys, and anything else new, into Callum's room was a process in itself. Due to his severely immune-compromised status, nothing was allowed entry that wasn't sterile. I mean nothing. If Trisha or I or one of the nurses had even the smallest cough, cold, or tickle in our throat, we couldn't be in Callum's room until it cleared. This wasn't just our rule, it was absolute for everyone on the eighth floor. Bringing a new toy, magazine, book, or videotape into a room on the hematology-oncology ward meant religiously sterilizing it beforehand. This involved scrubbing our hands, then scrubbing every inch of the suspect item with alcohol wipes before letting it dry. Only then was it ready to come in. Things we wanted to bring into his room later were keep in a clear, sterile garbage bag after being sterilized. If this seems crazy, it was.

By late afternoon, it was time for Trisha and me to switch places, with the changeover lasting until the following morning. Trisha blew Callum a kiss goodnight and took Thai back to RMH for dinner, and on the way they sometimes picked up groceries. RMH was a wonderful facility with TV rooms, craft rooms, and large shared kitchens where families could interact. Eventually, though, Trisha and I found it too hard to spend much time there. We were emotionally exhausted and sharing our story with new families every day didn't help. And it seemed like our child was always the sickest, which only increased our fears.

We spent a short time preparing dinner, then returned to our room to eat and have an early bedtime.

While Trisha was spending the night with Thai, I was at the hospital with Callum. Unlike during the day, we didn't play much. Callum was exhausted by evening, so instead we read lots of books and watched endless TV shows. A high point was calling to say goodnight to Mommy and Thai before bedtime. Then I turned the lights off and talked quietly to Callum as his eyes got heavy and closed. Finally, he slept, and I had three to five hours to myself to think, cry, hope for better days, and to find the strength to be the dad and husband Trisha, Callum, and Thai needed me to be. Those hours were very lonely. I emailed a lot. Sometimes I called family, but not that often and not for very long. As the evening stretched on, I watched television. I had a lot of difficulty falling asleep. It's weird to be exhausted and not be able to sleep. How I longed to fall asleep easily.

After a few weeks, I did find something to help me sleep. Turning off my mind was the real problem, and what helped was finding a reason to use it. I started studying again for my upcoming training exams in Emergency Medicine. These exams are held once a year in the spring over a three-day period. They're for all Royal College of Physician and Surgeons of Canada trainees in their last year of residency. The coming spring was my turn to write them. With work on hold, the furthest thing from my mind had been the practice of Emergency Medicine, but after talking things over with one of my medical school mentors while Thai and I were having dinner with his family, he convinced me to give studying a try, but with a caveat: to have no expectation of success. By telling me to not be afraid of failure, he gave me confidence. So I returned to my books for a few hours every night when Callum and Thai were sleeping. It kept my mind busy, gave structure to those lonely hours, and in the end made falling asleep a bit easier.

Having six hours or less of interrupted sleep on a small padded bench was extremely challenging and contributed to our mental, physical, and emotional fragility. While we realized there would always be issues when living in a hospital with a critically ill child, we were incredibly frustrated by the non-stop nighttime interruptions. We couldn't escape the background noises on the ward, the repeated beeping of the IV pump as it infused Callum overnight, and the seemingly constant pages on the overhead system. But there were other issues at Sick Kids that made these irritations harder to handle, the most consequential being the delivery of patient and family-centred care. We were benefitting from a very high level of expertise from numerous specialists, which was not available at Kingston General, but the minimal contact with the stem cell-transplant team – was a big change from the warm, frequent interactions we'd had with the oncology team at Kingston.

Despite the daily challenges, hearing "hi daddy" from Callum on those mornings we woke up together made most of it all better. First thing in the morning was when Callum was at his best. He had more energy and his mood was bright. His sweet hello transcended the fatigue, frustration, fear, and at times despair that I felt, and almost like a reversal of roles, when we woke up together it was like he was looking after me. Our morning ritual started with calling Mommy and Thai to say hi. Then Callum let me scoot down the hall to make toast and run downstairs to get a coffee. The Starbucks baristas greeted me with a smile and quickly prepared my tall Americano. On the way up the elevator, I inhaled the toast and drank half the coffee. By the six- or seven-minute mark I was setting my coffee on the table in the hallway outside Callum's room as I hurried to rejoin him. I would duck out later for 30 seconds to finish it off while he watched his morning TV show. Those first few hours together were the best. If we were lucky, the sun would be shining through the foyer windows. Soon Mommy would arrive after dropping Thai off at school.

On the weekends our routine changed a bit. Thai wasn't at school and the hospital was much quieter. Trisha and I took longer shifts away from each so we could spend more one-on-one time with Thai. Our family and friends would visit when they could. Those visits were to see Thai, Trisha and me since Callum wasn't allowed any visitors. Sometimes they lasted just a few hours and other times whoever had come stayed overnight at a hotel or in our small room at RMH.

Visiting with family and friends offered much needed support, but it was often stressful because we couldn't effectively communicate the grief, fear, pain, and exhaustion we were feeling. Watching Callum get sicker and sicker with each passing week was debilitating. Since our family wasn't able to see Callum and witness the progression of his illness, they couldn't form their own picture of the stark reality. They wanted everything to be okay, but nothing could be done to make it better and their hope and optimism didn't fit with what we were living. They often tried to convince Trisha and me to be easier on ourselves. We understood that the situation was hard on them too.

While Callum napped, I read the Saturday edition of the Globe and Mail from cover to cover. I read editorials, obituaries, and tributes. I read about politics, neighbourhoods, construction, and everything else. I learned a lot about Toronto and can still recall many of the feature stories. On Sundays, I did the same with the Toronto Star. When I was done, I often wrote a group email to update friends, family, and close colleagues. In the days that followed, I gravitated to my inbox to read everyone's replies and well wishes. The weekends also saw Thai and me venture further away from the hospital. He settled himself in the running stroller and off we went for one or two hours, sometimes covering up to twelve miles. As we toured the waterfront and areas such as High Park, Castlefrank, and Queen Street East, Thai eventually napped and I tried to be hopeful. A few times, we drove the half hour to Uncle Joel's house in Mississauga for a quick visit. Despite wanting to be with my older brother and his family, my heart rate went through the roof at being that far from Callum and Trisha. In the end, Thai and I only made two of those trips despite Joel's relative proximity.

I struggled to imagine how I would survive driving two hours away to attend the wedding of my little brother Vico at the end of September. We were just a few weeks into Callum's fourth cycle of chemotherapy, with the first stem cell transplant soon to follow, and I was scared of being out of town. But how could I miss my brother's wedding? Callum's condition seemed stable. Trisha's older sister Tracey said she would come to help out, which left me no choice. Trisha would have to be okay without me for twenty-four hours.

CHAPTER 5

Self-Pity, Hope, and Celebration

On a Friday afternoon in late September, Thai and I said goodbye to Trisha and Callum and got into our minivan to drive a few hundred kilometers to be with family and friends for Vico's wedding to Heather. Despite the light traffic, nice weather, and Thai being fast asleep in his booster seat in the back, I fought to keep myself together. It was hard to be alone with my thoughts. I was scared and the anxiety building inside of me was overwhelming. I knew I'd only be away from Callum for twenty-four hours, but it felt like an eternity. I couldn't stop thinking about something happening and me not being there. I tried as hard as I could to block this out of my mind, but with limited success.

Vico and Heather were close to Thai and Callum. Since they were both in medical school in Kingston while I was in residency, they had watched our boys grow up from the time they were infants. We shared many meals together and Uncle Vico was always game for being ridiculously silly and fun with his nephews. One of my favourite memories is of watching Callum and Vico ride a wooden stick horse through our house, galloping up and down the hallway, through the family room, then around the kitchen, their giggles and laughter never stopping. Eventually, Vico would run out of breath and the "horsie game" would come to an end.

Uncle Vico and Aunt Heather's wedding was supposed to be our first wedding with the boys. Thai and Callum had been very excited about it, and looked forward to getting dressed up in their little suits and participating in all the events. Trisha and I had been excited as well. We were so happy for Vico and Heather. They were a perfect pair and we were all going to have a great time celebrating with our families. But now our own family was only half there. Callum and Trisha were in isolation at Sick Kids dealing with the harsh realities of chemotherapy and having a stem cell transplant. This wasn't fair and I couldn't stop wallowing in self-pity as I drove along the highway. Everything was just so wrong.-

The only upside was that my two brothers, my sister Marla, and my parents would be waiting to see me. We had spent so much time away from each other over the past four months, it would be a relief to be hugged by them and to cry with them. Heather and her parents were also a great comfort, expressing genuine worry about Thai and me despite the next day's celebration. That first night, my siblings and I gathered in my hotel room to share some laughs and a few drinks. I had been figuratively holding my breath for four months, ever since hearing the words "brain tumour," and spending time with my family like that was something I really needed.

The next morning, I realized how exhausted and overwhelmed I was. I cried most of the day whenever I could find a few minutes away from everyone. As people started arriving at the hotel to get ready for the church service and wedding reception, I fought to keep it together. I spoke with Trisha on the phone and she settled me down, telling me she and Callum were fine. The nurses had said Callum's blood counts were much improved. The first stem cell transplant had worked. This was great news, but I couldn't stand not being there. The plan was for Thai and me to be back later that night.

When it was time for the wedding ceremony, I found whatever bit of strength was still inside of me and took a deep breath. This day was about Vico and Heather, I told myself, no more crying today, enough. On arriving at the church, Thai and I greeted everyone who was standing at the back. Thai, dressed in a tuxedo, handed the guests their programs with a huge smile. He was so happy and proud to be part of the big day. Normally very shy and reserved, he walked up the aisle with the procession and was the most confident I'd ever seen him. He was so handsome and acting like a big boy. I was bursting with pride and wished Trisha and Callum could be there to see him shine in his role.

At the reception, my siblings and I made a speech to welcome Heather into our family. We told jokes, all at Vico's expense, to let her know how happy we were she was taking him off our hands. By the time the after-dinner congratulations and speeches were finished it was 9 p.m., time to drive back to Toronto. But the events of the day had caught up with me and I knew it wouldn't be safe to drive two hours on the highway. I was exhausted. Instead, Thai and I said goodbye to everyone, returned to the hotel, packed our bags, and crawled into bed. We left for Sick Kids the next morning before everyone woke up. When we arrived at Callum's room, we were greeted with big smiles and excitement.

Trisha and Callum had a lot to tell us. While I was suffering because we were far away, they were celebrating with Aunt Tracey. They described how much fun they'd had on the day of the wedding. Callum had been allowed to leave his room because his blood counts were much better. I listened intently as Trisha described how he'd put on his facemask and galloped and scooted up the hallway wearing a huge smile. He was so excited to be able to leave his room. They played in the toy room and Callum drove around the hallway on his toddler bike. They had lots of fun and felt such joy. I was sad not to have been there for all those special moments, but it was more than okay. I was so happy for them.

For the first time all month, the four of us were allowed to be together and it was okay to touch Callum. We played all day that Sunday, and Trisha and I enjoyed watching our boys fool around with each other. We knew there were only a few days until this would be lost, as the next cycle of chemotherapy was starting on Wednesday. Callum would be exhausted and nauseous and throwing up again, and we would be trapped in the hospital room for another two to three weeks. At least we now had hope. We had two more rounds of chemotherapy, with each one followed by a stem cell transplant. Then we'd be done.

One of the things Callum and I liked to do during those days he was allowed out of his room was go downstairs to the atrium. The moment the nurses finished with his morning medications and infusions, he jumped on his scooter and I wasn't far behind, pushing his

IV pole. We made straight for the glass elevator, and Callum loved every minute of riding it down to the ground floor. He loved the way people winked at him as he pushed himself along on his scooter. With its four wheels and six-inch clearance, it was perfect for his weakened state, but it was also something any two-year-old would ride. Holding tight to the steering wheel, he zoomed along while I kept up behind him. When he got tired, he put his feet on the steering wheel and I pushed the scooter with the IV pole. We covered a lot of distance with this set-up.

Our usual routine was to start at the water fountain. I always came prepared with a loonie, which I traded with the cafeteria cashier for a roll of pennies. This gave Callum 100 throws into the fountain. He usually threw the first few dozen, then got tired and asked me to throw the rest. We invented many games around throwing those pennies, and we also made wishes to grow up big and strong, to travel the world, and to feel better once his chemotherapy was over. One day, I saw a man watching us. I smiled at him and he smiled back. He was close enough to hear our laughter and the wishes we were making. He could also see how small and fragile Callum was. When we were done, we walked past him and he said hi to me. Then he said, "I've been watching you and your son for the last ten minutes. I haven't been able to take my eyes off you. I know this may seem out of place, but you're a great dad. You really are." I smiled and said thank you, and a few tears streamed down my cheeks. As we walked away, Callum asked who the nice man was. I said, "He's a daddy too."

After throwing pennies, we always stopped at the toy store to look in the window at all the fun things. Callum would ask for the biggest toys he could see and I would promise him a surprise later in the day. It's funny how a little $2.99 toy brought him as much joy as something bigger and more expensive. As long as it could be sterilized with alcohol wipes, it could come into his room. Over time, Callum developed a collection of small toys that he carefully placed at the end of his bed.

Following our window shopping, we often picked up a coffee for Daddy at Starbucks. The baristas who had gotten to know me during the previous weeks were wonderful with Callum. They were fun and cheerful and spoiled him in any way they could. One of the ways was to give him coffee stickers from brews around the world to stick on his scooter. He thought this was very cool and hip. His bike now looked like the roof carrier on our car, full of colourful, tacky stickers from around the world. It really was a treat to sit and have a coffee with him for a few moments. We enjoyed being in each other's company outside of his hospital room.

After twenty minutes of being out and about, which usually included playing with the talking Cookie Monster garbage can and watching people come and go, it was time to return to his room. This small amount of activity exhausted Callum, and it was smart to recognize the moment when we should take the elevator back up to Callum's room. Callum's feet rested on his scooter as I pushed it with the IV pole. Usually within minutes of getting back in bed, he fell asleep and napped for an hour or two. I then sat beside the bed and stared at him for long periods of time, thinking how happy I was to be with him and how proud I was of his bravery and capacity for joy.

As planned, the fifth cycle of chemotherapy started just a few days after recovering from the previous one. We explained to the boys that we had to do this two more times. We said we were sorry that the four of us would be lonely for each other again, but we had to keep going. It was hard to know if they understood. On the first day of that cycle, Callum started vomiting almost immediately. In between bouts, he looked up at me and said, "Daddy, I have to get medicine to be sick so I can get better. Right Daddy?" Oh, how I wanted to cry with pride. Callum had heard Trisha and me and understood. He had to have all this horrible chemotherapy, endure his symptoms, and be attached to multiple lines and tubes to get better. He got what two more times meant, not two more days, but two more cycles. I was so proud of how smart and understanding and accepting he was. He couldn't have been more perfect.

Over the course of his surgery, chemotherapy, stem cell transplants, and IV infusions, many nurses, doctors, and social workers told us how wonderful Callum was. He said thank you to the nurses when they changed his central line and G-tube dressings when many other children screamed, cried, or fought. He smiled and said hi to them as they entered his room, though he was very sick and couldn't get out of bed. The many times we went for tests and procedures, he never cried or "put the brakes on," not even when we went to the operating room that first week at Sick Kids. If I told him it was okay or Trisha told him it was okay, he was okay. It was that simple. He trusted Trisha and me with absolute confidence. This made taking care of him far easier than it could have been.

As a doctor who works in the Emergency Room, I'm quite comfortable caring for children who kick, scream, cry, punch, push, thrash, and generally try to get as far away from me as possible. I smile when I think of the last five-year-old who kicked and yelled at me. I had asked him where his tummy hurt, and then I examined him there. To his mother's horror, he kicked me as hard as he could in my stomach. I thought his behaviour was appropriate. I smiled and said, "Sorry about that, honey. I had to push there to see how to make you better. Sorry I hurt you." He became much happier when I apologized and the rest of our interaction went smoothly. In my experience, children are more tolerant of procedures in the ER, even painful ones, when they feel safe, secure, and have some idea of what's happening. As Callum's daddy, my medical training really helped me to make him more comfortable and accepting about what was going on.

As an early childhood educator and primary school teacher, Trisha was just as comfortable managing children as I was, especially little ones. For years she studied about, then worked with, children between the ages of one and seven. Like me, she was used to kids kicking, screaming, crying, yelling, running away, and misbehaving in general. She taught me that children are much smarter than most adults give them credit for, and that consistent routines and expectations are essential to raising them to be happy and well-adjusted. Ultimately, parents make the rules and lead the way. Children will follow Mom and Dad's lead.

We maintained our belief in consistent routines and expectations with Callum and Thai, even though our home had become our rooms at Sick Kids and Ronald McDonald House, the four of us were often separated, and Callum's cancer scared the shit out of all of us. We still had expectations for them to be as good as possible, just as we would have if we were living our regular lives at home. We didn't let them off the hook. It was okay for Callum to be frightened, have pain, cry, and express himself in any way he needed to, as long as it wasn't hurtful to someone else.

Our family sometimes disagreed with this approach. Out of love, they thought we had taken on too much by putting Thai in school and being at Callum's bedside twenty-four hours a day. They thought we weren't giving ourselves enough time to rest. We knew what they were saying, especially when it was our parents talking, but Trisha and I were committed to controlling the few things we could. Thai needed to be with the three of us and to have structure. He needed to know we expected good behaviour from him and that he wasn't allowed to capitalize on his grandparents' lenient ways. Letting the boys' behaviour spiral out of control because we were tired wasn't an option we were interested in, even if it was harder on us. We firmly believed that parenting them in Toronto like we parented them at home would help them cope.

At times, it was tough to keep up this approach but we had a lot of support. Even though we were alone most of the time, we were always aware there was a "village of people" near and far who were worried about us. In addition to our family, who visited and called as frequently as they could, we received a constant stream of emails and letters, and from time to time friends came to meet us in the ground-floor atrium. Some lived in Toronto and others drove hundreds of kilometres to get there. Though this didn't happen often and the visits weren't very long, they were a much needed connection to the outside world.

Sometimes the visits happened during a weekday, but mostly they occurred in the evenings or on weekends when people could be away from work. Whenever it was, being able to make eye contact with old friends who knew us so well that we didn't need many words to communicate our anxiety and fears was important. I remember the grave looks on the faces of some of my friends as they listened to me tell them what was going on. These friends and these meetings, and even the toys they brought for the kids, were special and will never be forgotten.

One day, when I was returning from one of those atrium visits, I heard Code Blue announced on the paging system. It was for a teenager in a room down the hall from Callum who was undergoing chemotherapy for leukemia. In hospital language, Code Blue signals cardiac arrest or another life-threatening emergency. It prompts a systematic response from doctors, nurses, and respiratory therapists. Without quick action by this specialized team, the patient won't survive. Even when everything is done as fast and competently as possible, it's not unusual for patients to die because their body is too weak or sick to be resuscitated.

I watched from afar as the Code Blue team arrived and took control of the situation. I saw the child's parents crying in the hallway and selfishly thought, It could have been Callum. In that instant I was reminded of the precarious position he was in. He, too, was at risk of dire complications and a Code Blue being called for him. How would we get through all his treatments without his condition deteriorating further? A few minutes went by as I stood there with my thoughts, and now the team was racing the boy, who'd been strapped to a stretcher, towards the elevator in front of Callum's room. They were using a breathing mask with high-flow oxygen and he had several IV lines with medications running, in addition to the cardiac monitors attached to him. I heard the team leader say, "We're going to the ICU.

The patient is septic and had a respiratory arrest. He'll need to be intubated and we need to start pressors."

I thought to myself, Please let us stay up here. Don't let us go to the ICU. Don't let that happen to us. Please just let us spend two more months up here. We can handle that. Please! Please! I had a horrible feeling that if Callum went to the ICU, it meant we were losing the battle and he would die. To stay out of the ICU, I would do anything.

Seeing this incident made me wonder about Nicola, Callum's adorable two-year-old neighbour next door. Nicola had been transferred to the ICU a week ago and I hadn't heard how she was doing. She was a beautiful little girl with a blonde, fuzzy, mostly bald head, brown eyes, and chubby Italian cheeks. Lying there on her bed, she was as perfect as Callum was. I became worried and wondered if one of the nurses might know how things were going. I reminded myself that the staff wasn't allowed to tell us anything due to patient confidentiality, but after the Code Blue, I couldn't help myself. I wandered down the hall and approached a parent who seemed to know everything about everyone. She told me that Nicola had died a few days earlier, on September 24, of a complication related to her bone marrow transplant. That was the day Trisha and Callum were celebrating, the same day I was full of self-pity at my brother's wedding.

Trisha and I had met Judi, Carmine, and Nicola in the first or second week of September. I liked them right away. Nicola was the same age as Callum and was the youngest of three girls. Carmine was a softie and Judi was my favourite kind of woman – sweet and tough. Despite her small stature and lovely demeanor, she got my attention right away with her kind, genuine, and direct manner. The first day we met, Judi handed me tickets to a Toronto Blue Jays game. I learned quickly that saying "no thank you" to Judi wasn't an option. She said, "Go with Thai. He needs to have fun too." She was right. Thai had fun with the spectacle of it all, the fans, the game, the hot dogs and pop, the mascot, and the open-dome stadium with the sun shining through. I could see exactly what Judi meant. As much as possible, we needed to find a way to live that was more than the hospital, no matter how brief the moments. If we couldn't do it for ourselves, we needed to do it for Thai.

Judi taught me another lesson, this one about finding the courage to be who we were as a family. A few days after the ballgame, after complimenting me on what a beautiful family we were and how wonderful Callum was to play so patiently on his bed every day, she turned to me and said, "Everyone wants to see Callum's smiling face when he was well. Especially the nurses and doctors need to know who he is as a happy child at home, not just who he is when he's sick. Show us he's more than what's happening here. It's important for everyone to see past his illness." She suggested putting up pictures of him from when he was healthy. "Let us see him happy and lively and as perfect as he was before he became a cancer patient." I'm forever indebted to Judi's friendship and guidance.

Later that week, Nicola's condition worsened. That's when she went to the ICU. Trisha and I were so sad and scared to learn that she died. We couldn't imagine Judi and Carmine and their other two girls having to go home without their perfect angel.

The next two weeks were a blur. We continued our routine of alternating between staying with Callum at the hospital and shuttling Thai to school. We tried to keep focused on getting to the YMCA to exercise and have a shower, shopping for groceries, and waiting for another cycle to finish. Chemotherapy and its terrible side effects, including dangerously low white cell counts, once again defined our lives, as did the isolation, the transfusions, and the upcoming stem cell transplant. Though everything seemed a bit worse this time, we were inching closer to the sixth and last chemotherapy cycle. We were doing our best to take one day, one week, and one cycle at a time. We didn't want to get ahead of ourselves.

Although we weren't allowed to hug or kiss Callum for weeks at a time, I learned there was one exception to this rule. Sometimes, when I was lucky, I had the opportunity to hold him for a few minutes. Two or three times a week, Callum was required to have a quick bath in his room. If I chose to, I was allowed to be the one to bathe him without the help of his nurses. Those baths were wonderful and horrible at the same time.

The term bittersweet doesn't quite capture those moments. It was so much harder than that. Callum was exhausted and frail, and he was always cold when he wasn't wearing clothes or covered in blankets. Although almost three years old, he weighed just eighteen pounds. He had a central IV catheter line in his chest and a gastric tube in his abdomen that often really hurt. Getting him undressed, keeping him warm, minimizing his pain while carrying him, and maintaining absolute sterile conditions between his bed and the tub and then back again was challenging. Involving the nurses was an option, but I didn't want to. I knew they were there if needed, but I longed for the intimacy of being alone with Callum, even if it was only for ten minutes.

The baths went like this: With Callum in his bed, I bundled him up in lots of blankets so he'd become as warm as possible. Then I went to the nursing station to get a stack of sterile towels and a sterile washcloth. Back in his room, I placed the towels and washcloth on the side of the tub, which I'd already wiped with alcohol swabs. After carefully unbuttoning Callum's pajama shirt, removing most of his dressings, and taking off his bottoms, I carried him, in his train-themed pull-ups, to the side of the tub. He would be shivering as I removed his pull-up and placed his fragile body, with catheter lines sticking out of his abdomen and chest, into the water. Quickly and gently, I cleaned his body with the wet washcloth, being careful not to overly soak the dressings for his lines.

Within a minute of being in the tub, Callum asked if he could get out. Gingerly, I stood him on a sterile towel on the floor. I sat down on the nearby toilet, placed a towel on my lap, and gently placed him on the towel and wrapped his body with two more. For two minutes

I held him there, and because he couldn't see me, I cried. Tears rushed down my face. I couldn't believe how touching him filled my heart with joy and anguish at the same time. I then moved us to the sterile towels on the bench, where his fresh pull-up and pajamas lay. After getting him dressed as carefully and quickly as possible, I held him again for a few minutes before putting him back in bed. By this time, Callum was exhausted and soon fell asleep. As he slept, I gazed at him and quietly cried.

On waking from his nap, Callum needed clean dressings for the tubes in his chest and abdomen that delivered medications and nutrition to his body. He made me proud every time this happened. He never cried, instead, he often talked with the nurse as she worked, though sometimes the dressings would stick to his dry, hypersensitive skin. When she was done, Callum invariably said thank you without being prompted. Unfailingly, the nurse would say, "Wow, he's so good. Is he always like this? Most kids on our ward are afraid of dressing changes, especially at his age." Each time, my response was a very proud, "Yes, he's always this good."

Thai also made us endlessly proud. As a baby, he was happy and secure. From the first moment Trisha and I held him in our arms, he showed a calmness and contentment that never wavered. So it was no surprise that he faced his brother's illness with patience, understanding, and good behaviour, despite all the attention Callum received. He accepted that he had only limited opportunities to play with his brother. He didn't fuss about Callum's chemotherapy cycles or his isolation or that we were living in a small room at RMH. When I think of all the times Thai missed a nap so we could do errands for Mommy and Callum at the hospital, sometimes going much further than expected in the running stroller, I'm amazed at his quiet composure. It was the same when I extended his bedtime so I could have a rare visit with family or friends. At least a few times a week, I pushed the limits of what any four-year-old could handle, but Thai would lay his head in my lap or on my shoulder and fall asleep without tears or drama. His response to our difficult new world was incredibly helpful.

As the fifth cycle of chemotherapy and the second stem cell transplant were coming to an end, I found myself daydreaming about the four of us being home again. If things went well, we would be in Kingston by the end of November or early December. But I kept these daydreams short. Callum still had a lot to get through with cycle six and his last stem cell transplant. I was conscious of what he'd endured so far and the life-threatening complications that could happen at any time. His body had become much more fragile with each passing week and I couldn't bear to think of him enduring another grueling and dangerous round of chemotherapy. I was filled with such anxiety and fear that I couldn't talk out loud about Callum going home until the time came. In a few weeks I would let myself think of the next phase – recovery.

CHAPTER 6

Then It All Changed

As much as we needed to take one day at a time until we were in the clear, with only a few weeks until the final stem cell transplant was over, it was time to start thinking about home. We cautiously sketched out a transition plan. Callum would recover at Kingston General after his discharge from Sick Kids, and Thai would need help preparing to re-enter his old school. I thought about when I'd go back to work. Callum's immune system would be significantly weakened for many months and maybe years, and we were advised to remove all the carpets and old flooring in our house to minimize his exposure to germs and allergens. While the four of us were still in Toronto, our family and friends started the renovations.

The days leading up to Callum's final cycle of chemotherapy were precious. We played and laughed all day long. We talked with our family about the possibility of being home together in time for Christmas. The day before chemotherapy began, Callum and Thai went to the playroom on the eleventh floor, excited to be in each other's company. Most of their time was spent at the Thomas the Train table, maneuvering the trains up and down the tracks and seeing how many of the cars they could connect. All of a sudden, Callum lay down in the middle of the room on a mat. He told me he felt sick, but he wanted to stay there so he could be with Thai. The doctor in me wondered what kind of complication was affecting what organ system or systems to cause this. I waited a few minutes, then carried him to his room and put him in bed. Almost right away he vomited, then he told me his back hurt, which was a new complaint. I watched him fall asleep.

We hadn't even started the last cycle of chemo and he was the weakest he'd ever been. That night I cried so hard while he slept. I wished with everything in me that this stupid goddamn cycle of dreadful chemo would be over and we could go home. It was unbearable to see him suffer so much. After waking from his nap, Callum and I made our last trip to the atrium to throw pennies into the fountain, visit the talking garbage can, and chat with our Starbuck's friends. He was too tired to throw the pennies so I threw them in one by one as we made wishes together. We wished for another trip to Disney World, to one day visit Italy and Hawaii, to feel better, to grow bigger like Daddy, to go home together soon, and to swim at our favourite community pool.

Before returning to the eleventh floor, we decided to get an Oreo ice cream sandwich from the cafeteria. For weeks, Callum had been receiving his nutrition from a gastric feeding tube and rarely, if ever, ate food by mouth. Even knowing he would have only a bite or two, he was so excited. He took a tiny nibble, licked the ice cream, then gave the rest of it to me. He was so proud of himself for eating something.

The start of cycle six the next day brought with it a return to our strict isolation protocol and Callum vomiting repeatedly. Every day, his fatigue became worse. The bathtimes we shared became fewer and further between as any movement was too painful and made him vomit instantly. His skin had turned an ominous waxy grey. He slept more than ever and his days were defined by watching TV and Trisha and me reading books to him. The games we'd played during earlier cycles were now too taxing for him. Instead, we played pretend and dreamed about him growing bigger and stronger once his medicine was done. To make him smile, I impersonated as many characters as I could think of from the shows we watched. Oscar the Grouch, Cookie Monster (my personal favourite), Max, Ruby, Dora, Diego, and Blue and Mailbox from Blue's Clues. We talked about the fun times he and Thai would have soon. Sometimes, as a treat, Silly Sally, the Sick Kids clown, stopped by for a visit. Callum loved her and she was truly great at responding to his need for quiet play. Those fifteen-minute visits from Silly Sally really lifted our spirits for a couple of hours after she left.

As the sixth cycle progressed, Callum experienced pain and symptoms that he hadn't before. Trisha and I were reaching our breaking point. The frustrations of being away from home for so long and isolated from family and friends, and being powerless to find solutions to the day-to-day struggles of living in the hospital, were becoming too much. Callum's new symptoms, on top of his profound fatigue and frequent vomiting, included pain in his back and bum, poor sleep at night, and general body aches. He told us that all his bones hurt. For a child who was about to turn three, it wasn't easy for him to find the exact words to communicate what the problem was, but Trisha and I could tell that things were different. We knew his body was barely holding on.

Spending nearly every minute of every day with him, we had the feeling we were too close to a dangerous clifftop. Everything seemed worse. His body was so frail. Those days were the only times I pleaded with God. I wouldn't say I prayed in the traditional manner. I asked, begged, and bargained for help in getting us through the next few weeks. I longed, as did Trisha, to take Callum's place in that bed. If only it were our bones aching and our bodies vomiting. If only it was one of us dying and not Callum. That would have been better than what we were facing with our baby.

Just sitting up in bed was starting to be uncomfortable for Callum. Pain medications didn't seem to do anything. Wanting to soothe him, I doused a cloth in cold water and lay it on his back and buttocks. Often this helped enough to allow him to nap. Looking back, I realize his new pain was caused by swelling in his liver, the chemotherapy breaking down his bones, and his lungs starting to fill with fluid. As all this progressed, so did his pain.

Everything started to snowball. The deterioration of Callum's health combined with our fear that he was dying and five months of living in hospital with its non-stop interruptions was overtaking us. We were increasingly scared, exhausted, frustrated, and impatient when our simplest needs weren't met. It's hard to describe the strain of trying to sleep at night when Callum was suffering beside me, his infusion pump beeping every hour to be reset and the paging system going off every half hour. As each day passed, falling asleep became harder and staying asleep, impossible. All we could accomplish between 1 a.m. and sunrise were short stretches of stupor-like sleep that didn't amount to much. Trisha and I were both aware of the toll this was taking. We struggled to deal with the challenging setting and the ongoing high-stakes decisions and treatments, but we were barely hanging on.

Other issues contributed to our fear and frustration, like poor medical team interactions, errors with medication, and significant breaks in sterile technique. One encounter in particular combined three types of errors: medication, administrative, and communication. With each cycle, Callum needed antifungal medication because his risk of infection was so high. Without it, he could easily contract a serious systemic infection that could kill him, or it could interfere with the chemotherapy's action, as had happened recently to another child on our floor who was receiving a similar type of chemotherapy protocol. Not knowing if he had gotten the appropriate antifungal medication the week before, Trisha asked the nurse one evening to check. The nurse did, then returned to say she couldn't find any record of it. After calling me to ask what to do, Trisha explained to the nurse the importance of the medication and asked her to page the resident physician on-call.

Sometime later, the resident physician arrived in Callum's room. She told Trisha that the medication had probably been administered and everything was fine. Trisha explained that the stem cell transplant team had been adamant that it needed to be given during a specific window of time to be effective and so it would not interfere with the action of the chemotherapy. The resident continued with her efforts to be reassuring, repeating that everything was probably okay. Trisha kept asking for certainty. Had Callum received the medication or not? She then asked the resident to call the attending physician for his opinion. Her response was that she was the senior resident and her opinion was that Callum was fine, and the situation could be dealt with the next day. Fed up, Trisha explained that she was married to a senior ER resident and he didn't know everything either and sometimes had to call the attending physician for help. This was a simple problem the attending physician likely knew the answer to. She then said she wouldn't take no for an answer.

Shocked, the senior resident physician left the room. She returned later to say that after making a few calls, including one to a nurse at her home, she could say with certainty that Callum had received the medication the week before at the right time. It hadn't been charted, but she guaranteed it had been given. With that, Trisha thanked her for resolving the issue, but the conflict had left her feeling terribly unsettled.

Medication errors happen every day in hospitals around the world. That's the truth. Giving the wrong drug or dose, being unaware of the side effects of a drug or how it might negatively interact with other drugs, administering a drug through the wrong route or at the wrong time or for the wrong duration, are just a few examples. Mistakes happen, but when a team's response to a parent pointing out a real or possible error is indifference, defensiveness, and avoidance, there's a bigger problem. Trisha and I were already struggling with the fact of Callum being critically ill, and our patience, understanding, and willingness to forgive the staff for mistakes and defensive attitudes were disappearing. Were we overreacting? Was our fatigue and stress getting the best of us? Or were there larger system issues?

From our point of view – a combination of our experiences and the knowledge I had from my medical training – we knew the current system of treatment protocols, algorithms, and tracking medications needed to be better. It seemed obvious that it should be fully computerized and automated, with appropriate prompts and checks from the pharmacy. There also needed to be computerized sign-offs by healthcare personnel when medications or treatments were completed. Extremely complicated protocols demanded a high level of safety checks, duplication, and redundancy, like the safety protocols in aviation, but as far as we could tell, this kind of system didn't exist yet in medicine. A better system would curtail the fear of trainees asking for help, encourage better supervision by team leaders, help healthcare workers track complex individualized care plans, and reduce the medical vigilance required by stressed-out parents who should be focused on being present with their child and each other. Thankfully, since our time at Sick Kids, many patient safety initiatives have been implemented to optimize care.

At this point in Callum's treatment, he was getting sicker by the day. Just as Dr. Bartels had told us back in June, the chemotherapy protocol had become increasingly dangerous. Two weeks after starting cycle six, Callum's blood counts were again decimated, which meant he needed daily transfusions of red blood cells and platelets. His white blood cells, barely measureable on routine blood work, were almost non-existent. He needed one last stem cell transplant to rescue his body from the very real risk of dying from the multitude of infections that could overwhelm him in this vulnearable state.

The day before the sixth stem cell transplant was Callum's third birthday – October 24, 2006. With the permission of the medical team, we arranged to have a cake made and he was allowed to invite some of his new friends from the ward, along with their parents, to celebrate with him at a brief party in a separate isolation room. We were especially excited because Thai would be able to be with his brother for a whole day, maybe two. Despite Callum being frail, exhausted, and looking sicker than we'd ever seen him, his spirits were high. He was so excited to have a birthday party for his "real birthday," no matter how short it would be. That my dad was back in town and would join the four of us made me particularly happy.

The forecast called for a sunny day and all of us were filled with excitement. I really had to contain my thoughts, though. I hadn't had this much hope in a long time. Not only were we celebrating Callum's birthday, within a week his blood counts would start going up. When that happened, a few weeks later we would go home. I felt like the worst of the worst would soon be over, and every day would bring new hope and promise.

Arriving in Callum's room on the morning of the party shattered that hope. His colour was a combination of grey, black, blue, and white. His face was gaunt and dark, despite his smile. His skin was thin and waxy and partially mottled. He looked dramatically worse than he had the night before. My dad was with me, and on entering the room he had to leave almost immediately so Callum wouldn't see him cry. In the hallway, we hugged each other because we couldn't bear to see Callum look so sick. But that wasn't my son's frame of mind. Despite his appearance, his spirits were unbroken. He was happy and excited.

Later that morning, right on cue, Callum's cake arrived along with his ward friends and their parents, several nurses, and everybody else who'd gotten to know him in the last few months. He was overjoyed to be in a room with other children. Being in isolation was so hard. Watching his face, we could see how much he'd longed to play with friends and be around people. He'd always been a busy, outgoing, happy child. Regardless of all his physical ailments, the essence of who he was remained intact. Trisha and I were very proud of how special he was. We couldn't have asked any more of him in that moment.

We couldn't have real birthday candles, so when the time came to blow them out, we pretended. Then we cut the cake. Everybody got a piece and we all dug in, except for Callum. He tried to lift a small bite of cake to his mouth but couldn't. Just trying to sit up made him nauseated, so eating, even something so good, was out of the question. He put it down and asked Trisha to take it away. He continued to be happy and content, though. He knew he was loved by everyone and he made the best of the situation. That day, Callum, who had just turned three years old, taught us a lesson in courage, acceptance, and strength.

A short time later, he was moved back to his regular room, where he was connected to cardiac, respiratory, and temperature monitors, all part of the strict protocol the nurses and physicians had to follow that afternoon. Soon, in one last stem cell transplant, his own stem cells would be re-infused into his body. Trisha stayed with Callum while Thai and I went back to Ronald McDonald House to have a quiet afternoon. We had recently moved to a different room that was bigger and more comfortable. Thai had a small play area for his cars and train set and I had a spot where I could exercise in front of the TV beside him. As we settled in, I thought of Trisha and Callum settling in for a busy afternoon at the hospital.

Then it all changed. I called Trisha to check in because of how unwell Callum had looked that morning, and that was the moment the panic started. "Something's wrong," she said. "They put him on oxygen. They're all worried. I'm not sure what's happening. Callum's sitting in bed okay but something's definitely wrong." She told me they'd said something about his oxygen levels being in the 70s, and that since they hadn't checked his levels in over a week, they didn't know how long they'd been that low. "Damon, I'm scared."

At that moment, I became completely unravelled. I could no longer contain my mind or emotions. I couldn't breathe. My heart raced and I wanted to throw up. I wanted to give way to my panic and let myself cry and scream. The possibility of Callum dying now, not later, became real. Everything suddenly made sense: his terrible colour and new back pain, his difficulties breathing, a grunting sound he'd started to make in the last week. His lungs had been struggling and maybe his heart too. Was this an infection? Was it heart and lung toxicity from the chemotherapy? There were so many possibilities that could explain his deterioration, some of them life-threatening. From that moment on, we were in a very different place.

How long before he was taken to the ICU? Was it possible he could stop getting sicker or was I deluding myself? There was a reason we'd become more scared of the chemotherapy than the brain tumour. Back in June and again in August, the oncologists and transplant specialists at Sick Kids had told us that no child Callum's age, with his type of tumour, had been cured. His treatment, with the hope of saving him, demanded pushing his body – and his life – to the limit. Now I didn't know if it was too late for the last stem cell transplant to rescue him this time.

We lived through the next week tormented by terrible anxiety, worry, and stress. As my mind and emotions became increasingly unstable, each day hurt more than the previous one. Trisha and I were doing our best to hold it together, but the effects of this very real threat made us suffer to an almost unbearable degree. To keep Callum's blood oxygen saturation at a safe level, he went from receiving oxygen by nasal prongs to wearing a mask. More than ever, he was imprisoned in his own bed. All Trisha and I could do was read books to him, watch TV with him, talk to him as he fell asleep, and keep him from seeing us crumble around him.

During that week, there were more frequent visits by the doctors and nurses, but no one had a clear understanding of what was going on in Callum's body. Infection from rare bacteria or fungus, or both, was the biggest concern. After that, maybe toxicity from the chemotherapy had damaged his heart, lungs, liver, and, possibly, his kidneys. Callum underwent blood work and a number of tests, including chest X-rays, a CT scan, and a bronchoscopy under anaesthesia in the operating room. We were hoping they would yield an answer. If not, the reason for his deterioration would be much more worrisome and only time would tell if his body would go into respiratory failure. If he couldn't breathe on his own, there would be nothing the team could do to reverse it.

All the very best medicine and technology could do was support Callum's body as it worked to survive the crisis. Whatever damage was done couldn't be undone by either medications or machine. Knowing this harsh reality, we were hoping the culprit was some type of rare fungal infection in his lungs that could be treated with powerful drugs. This was exactly the type of infection the doctors had been trying to prevent for the last five months and until now we'd been terribly afraid of.

A few days after being put on oxygen, Callum was taken to the OR for the broncoscopy. This involved being put asleep by an anaesthetist and having a lung specialist put a tube with a camera down his throat and into his lungs to examine his tissues and take samples. It was a straightforward procedure and on its own nothing to particularly worry about. Plus we'd been to the OR before, for Callum's neurosurgery in June, which had focused our minds with its immediate purpose and outcome. But this procedure and OR visit was different. Callum had endured five months of chemotherapy and all the complications that came with it. As a result, he was a frail version of his former self. Trisha and I were frail as well and couldn't hide our fears as we had before.

I remember trembling as the doctors spoke to us in the pre-operative suite. It was evening and I could barely keep it together after another long, stressful day. I didn't cry, but I was aware of being at my emotional limit. I remember nodding along with Trisha to the instructions they gave us. Then we were briefed again on what they were doing and why, the potential complications, and what the next steps would be depending on the results. I was asked if I would like to accompany Callum to the OR to settle him in. I said yes.

As I walked down the hall with Callum on a stretcher at my side, I gave myself a pep talk. More than anything, I wanted to focus all my calm and loving attention on him until the moment he fell asleep. We stepped into the OR and my focus faltered. Callum was scared like I'd never seen before. He started to cry and it crushed me. He had been through so much pain and fatigue and discomfort, always with patience and a smile, that I wasn't ready for his tears. I couldn't shield him from the fear that overwhelmed my face. I had no smiles to give him. He knew this was bad.

Still crying, he reached up to me with his arms, asking me to pick him up and take him to his room. Now tears were streaming down my face. I said, "I'm sorry, honey, just one more test, sweetheart. Mommy and I will be here when you wake up." I looked up at the anaesthetist and was overtaken by a feeling of helplessness. She quickly started the sequence of putting Callum to sleep. He closed his eyes and I left the operating room. I was filled with guilt, anger, agony, and fear as I walked down the hallway to the waiting room. When Trisha's eyes met mine, I broke down completely. I was more afraid at that moment than I'd ever been. I remember thinking, Is this the beginning of the end?

Over the next three days, we got the results from the blood work, bronchoscopy, CT scan, and chest X-ray. They were normal or inconclusive. The doctors still had no answer to the question of what was causing Callum's worsening condition. In the meantime, his oxygen requirement was slowly increasing and I felt that being transferred to the ICU was inevitable. As Trisha and I prepared ourselves, we tried to protect Thai from our escalating pain and decreasing ability to function. He was only four and a half years old and he needed us, but we were no longer able to focus on anything but Callum and each other. Trisha's parents and my dad agreed to come to Toronto to look after Thai, which meant we could both be at the hospital night and day.

On the day Nana and Papa were to arrive, I picked Thai up from school for the last time. There he was in the playground, running around with his classmates, having fun, with his teacher looking on from the school steps. As usual, I let him have a few extra minutes with his friends before we left for the day. I loved watching him play when he didn't know I was there. It let me know how happy he was and that he was doing okay, despite living at Sick Kids and RMH because his little brother had cancer.

As I watched, Thai's teacher walked over to check in. Instead of quickly wiping the tears from my face as I usually did before saying hi, I let them stay. I told him things weren't good, that Callum's condition had taken a turn for the worse. I explained how much it mattered to me that Thai was learning and having fun at school, and how hard it had been to get him there the last few days. He listened intently, then told me how special Thai was, both as a student and a friend to his classmates. He reassured me that Thai was flourishing, and he hoped very much that Callum's condition would improve. I shared my fear that it wasn't going to. With fresh tears streaming down my face, I told him we might find ourselves in the ICU within the coming days and that Thai might not return to school. Everything was too uncertain. At that, Thai and I left the schoolyard and headed back to the hospital.

Finally, Nana and Papa arrived. Their presence allowed me to spend all my time with Trisha and Callum, but we were unable to help each other or him. All we could do was physically be in each other's company. We could protect Thai by leaving him with his grandparents, but the other three members of our family were trapped.

During this period, I was the only person who understood what was going on inside Trisha's head. I was attuned to her emotions, her thoughts, and her immediate needs. I knew that what she said didn't necessarily equate to how she felt or what she wanted. That was okay because I was used to reading her. We knew each other's looks and body language. Most of the time, words weren't really needed. Growing up together, being friends, dating in our early twenties, and being married for eight years meant that sometimes I knew her better than she knew herself. Now we were in full crisis mode and I would protect her as best I could with everything I had. What she really needed, though, I couldn't give her.

At this stage, worrying about ourselves didn't make sense. Every part of us was focused on Callum. Eating, sleeping, and talking with extended family and friends seemed irrelevant and was distracting and upsetting. I don't mean to make us sound cold. It's just the truth. We were spending our days with doctors who didn't know what was going on, and not because of lack of effort. It was possible that Callum was dying in front of us. We wouldn't let anything stand in the way of being with him for every minute of every day. This led to some very difficult moments with our family. At times, Trisha's parents, my parents, and our siblings struggled to accept our decisions. We didn't always agree about what was best for Thai, and they were worried we were neglecting the basic needs of our own health. As only loving parents can do, they asked us hard questions and pointed out where they thought we were going wrong. It was true, things were falling off the rails, but there was nothing anyone could do to make it better.

What I remember about those six months was that Trisha and I knew exactly what mattered to us, and that was our boys, each other, and the four of us as a family. That's why we took Thai to Toronto and spent so much time at the hospital. That's why we ignored the advice of family, friends, and medical personnel who as the weeks passed increasingly told us to take time away and pay better attention to our own health. I knew we were making decisions that others wouldn't have, but Thai and Callum were the centre of our world, and now Callum needed us even more. From the beginning, we'd leaned on our parents and siblings for all the help they could give. Now this meant asking them to take care of Thai full-time, which we realized was asking a lot. But we were terrified we were facing an ending and we weren't about to shy away from hard decisions.

Seven days passed with Callum getting oxygen by mask. Every day his condition worsened. Trapped in a downward spiral, I tried desperately to figure out what was causing his deterioration. Given that I was within months of my final training exam in Emergency Medicine, maybe I could think of something that would help. But I was his daddy, not his doctor, and his complicated treatment protocols were beyond my training.

Nonetheless, I pushed my mind hard to make sense of his condition. I struggled to process the possibilities. First principles suggested an undiagnosed lung infection with pulmonary bleeding, or possibly congestive heart failure. Chemotherapy could destroy cells in any organ. Had his lungs been damaged? Or worse, had his heart been damaged and this was the start of a toxic cardiomyopathy that would lead to cardiac and respiratory failure? If yes, any further deterioration would mean a one-way progression to cardiovascular failure. I couldn't allow myself to accept this thought until it was said out loud by one of the physicians. Until then, I wouldn't tell Trisha that this was a possibility, though she was already filled with fear that Callum was dying.

During the last evening I spent with Callum in his isolation room, I began to notice he was breathing harder despite his oxygen mask. Not only were his chest muscles moving faster, more muscles were engaged. His nostrils were flaring with each breath and I could hear his breathing change to a higher pitch. He was already on the maximum amount of oxygen by mask that could be delivered in his isolation room. He needed more, which meant having a breathing tube placed in his lungs. He also needed closer monitoring in an intensive care environment by doctors, nurses, and respiratory therapists with more experience. I knew the time had come to go to the ICU.

Early that evening, when the resident physician on-call came by to check on Callum's condition, it came up that I was in medicine too. So when at 2 a.m. I asked the nurse to tell him we needed to go to the ICU, he came promptly. I quickly explained my reasoning and that I could help him with the transport to the second floor, if needed. I was scared, but I had a job to do. Callum needed to get to the ICU before he stopped breathing and a Code Blue was called. The only physicians who would be comfortable managing this situation were in the ICU. I called Trisha at Ronald McDonald House to let her know, and moments later Callum and I were in the elevator with the nurse and resident physician, urgently en route.

CHAPTER 7

We're Losing the Fight

Trisha and I stood at the end of Callum's bed, scared out of our minds about what might come next. We held on tight to each other as we watched the team get our son settled in his new surroundings. More monitors were attached to him, oxygen-mask settings were adjusted, additional IV catheters were placed, and information was continuously exchanged between the team members. After a week of panicking about all the medical issues, I could now turn off the doctor part of my brain. I was surrounded by ICU nurses, respiratory therapists, and physicians who were skilled in pediatric resuscitation and critical illness. They would take care of Callum and I could focus on being his dad.

As the recipient of all this fussing about, Callum was calm and mostly oblivious to the change in circumstances. The staff spoke to him softly and made every effort to ensure he was okay. Now that he was receiving a higher oxygen flow and a small amount of pain medication, he was breathing bettter. The panic I'd felt earlier that evening was fading, but there was still no answer for why all this was happening. Soon Callum was comfortable enough to fall asleep. Trisha and I knew we should get some sleep too, but neither of us was prepared to leave the room. The nurse brought in a small cot and placed it in the corner. We both lay down and closed our eyes. This was the first time we'd slept in the same bed since early September.

By 7 a.m., we were all awake and about to learn a new ICU routine. Every morning there would be blood work, nursing handovers, rotating respiratory therapists, physician team rounds, and updates from the attending physician. He made a great first impression. He was gentle and confident, with an excellent bedside manner. He was also well versed in Callum's medical issues and history, and at our first meeting he spent extra time walking us through the care plan for the next twenty-four hours. He explained there would be meetings with specialists, examinations of the tests that had been conducted, and that additional IV antibiotics and other medications would be given until there were more answers.

Callum's breathing was the most concerning issue, but before deciding to intubate we would wait to see if it worsened. Trisha and I explained to the attending physician that Callum's older brother Thai would want to see him before he was sedated and a breathing tube inserted. We were worried that if things continued to get worse, Callum and Thai might never have the chance to talk with each other again. The doctor promised that he alone would make the decision and wouldn't proceed without discussing it with us first.

Over the course of the day, we let our family know that Callum was in the ICU. They made sure they were never more than a ten-minute walk from the hospital, rotating between Ronald McDonald House, the Sick Kids atrium, the ICU waiting room, and anywhere else that was close by. Trisha and I popped out a few times to see them and grab something to eat, but leaving Callum for even ten minutes made us increasingly uncomfortable. If things were going to get worse, nothing in this world was more important than being at his bedside. More than ever, we were withdrawing from everyone.

In the ICU, Callum was completely confined to his bed. He was attached to monitors and IV lines and wasn't able to do much of anything except watch TV and listen to Trisha and me read him stories. He was quiet and working hard to breathe. He didn't cry. He was accepting of his situation. Trisha and I knew that all we could do was give him our love in any way possible. At the same time, our hearts were breaking. Our fears of going to the ICU had come true. I couldn't shut out the thought that Callum was dying in front of us.

By the end of the first day, his condition hadn't worsened but it hadn't improved. He needed 60 percent oxygen by mask and there was no sign that his lungs were getting stronger. We knew what was coming. Callum would need a breathing tube within the next twenty-four hours, which meant being sedated so he could tolerate the discomfort. He wouldn't be able to talk. I was preparing myself mentally for this and trying to figure out how to explain it to Callum when the time came. This was bad, very bad. There would be no way to sugar-coat it. I decided to return to Callum's old room on the hematology-oncology ward to sleep for a few hours on the bench where either Trisha or I had slept for the last two months. It took everything in me to fall asleep. After waking up at 3 a.m. from a vivid nightmare of Callum dying, I made my way to the ICU. From that moment on, I never left him at night again. Any sleep I managed to get was on the cot, next to Trisha.

In the morning, I waited for the doctor to say that today was the day Callum would be intubated. At 9 a.m., he made it official, telling us that if things were no different by the afternoon, Callum would need a breathing tube and be attached to a ventilator. I asked what he thought was going on with his heart and lungs. We talked about the fluid buildup in his lungs, his low blood pressure and fast heart rate, and the interconnectedness of these medical issues. Because of Callum's weak heart, high oxygen need, and deteriorating condition, a breathing tube was unavoidable.

During our discussion, I didn't tell Callum's doctor that I was a physician. If he'd asked, I would have answered honestly, but I purposefully withheld that I was in the same profession because I wanted to be only a dad. I worried that if the medical team knew, they would feel like I was asking for special treatment. Another worry I had was that they would direct the updates at me and unintentionally leave Trisha out of the discussions. This had happened previously during Callum's illness and I wanted to avoid it now. It was important to me that our family be treated the same as the other families in the ICU.

In the afternoon, Trisha stepped out to get something to eat with her family. It was a long overdue break. Shortly after she left, a new attending physician arrived and decided that a different oxygen mask, called a BiPAP, might help Callum's breathing. I tried to explain to him that a plan was already in place that the other attending physician had made with us, but this attending physician felt differently. He then left the room. Trisha had just gone for a break, and at the time, I didn't think I needed to call her cellphone to give her an update. With a resident physician and a respiratory therapist standing by, I explained to Callum how the new mask would push air into his lungs. As it was placed on his face, I could see nothing but fear in his eyes. Right away I knew it wasn't going to work. Within seconds Callum started to panic. The machine required coordinated breathing, and even though I tried calmly to talk him through the next sixty seconds, he couldn't accept the feeling of air pushing into his lungs.

Suddenly, the BiPAP alarm went off. Almost immediately, Callum's blood pressure dropped to a dangerously low 55/30, and that alarm started ringing too. Then his oxygen-saturation alarm began to ring because his oxygen levels were falling, from 95 to 80, then to 70. After that the drop was immeasurable over a matter of seconds. At that point, Callum became unconscious and stopped breathing. He was now blue in the face and fingers.

I was frantic. I asked the resident physician to activate a Code Blue, then immediately went into doctor mode and helped the respiratory therapist take the mask off and reposition Callum. Then I assisted while he aggressively ventilated him with 100 percent O2 by bag-valve-mask. Over the next three minutes, Callum's colour improved, and as I checked for a pulse his oxygen-saturation reading climbed above 80, then to 85 and 90. All the while the respiratory therapist continued to forcefully ventilate his lungs. Moments later, Callum's systolic blood pressure registered on the monitors again and was above 60, but he was still unconscious. When the Code Blue team arrived, I stepped back from the bed and let them take over. Overwhelmed by the fact that Callum had nearly died, I wept.

The ICU attending physician who had been with us since the day before had heard the Code Blue, and by the time he entered the room Callum's vital signs were more stable. He guided me into an outer room and I watched the team care for Callum through a large window. I could see the attending physician giving them instructions. Everything seemed fairly calm, but Callum hadn't woken up yet. All I could think of was whether he would ever wake up again. Had his heart really stopped beating in front of me? I couldn't live without seeing him smile at me again and hearing him talk to me. What would I tell Trisha? Then I realized, Oh my God, Trisha's not here! A flood of panicked thoughts filled my head as I cried alone in the outer room.

Soon the attending physician let me know they would be going ahead with the intubation. I nodded. Now I wouldn't have the chance to explain it to Callum. Right at that moment, Trisha arrived. I tried to tell her what had happened, but I was crying too hard. I finally managed to say, "Callum's okay now, but he came close to dying." We held each other and cried. An hour later, Callum had a breathing tube in his throat and Trisha and I were seated at his bedside. He was awake and looking at us. He couldn't speak because of the tube and he was mildly sedated to help with the discomfort. From his expressions and his ability to nod yes and no, we could tell Callum was himself. He hadn't suffered any brain damage.

He didn't fuss about the tube. He just looked at us, and then he did something truly magical. Trisha had told him she loved him and was proud of him. He responded by using the fingers of his right hand to show her the "I love you" sign. Trisha had taught him this hand sign weeks earlier, but never imagined he would know to use it at a time like this, when it was one of the only ways he could communicate with us. Despite all that had happened, he continued to surprise and inspire us.

That night was a tough one. Trisha and I had cried many, many tears prior to arriving in the ICU, but starting when Callum was on the ventilator, our tears flowed more freely than ever. We didn't attempt to hide it and we didn't care who saw us. From his bed, Callum couldn't hear us crying in the corner, and Thai wasn't with us. From then on, Trisha and I stayed together 24/7, which we hadn't done since Callum was diagnosed in June. Seeing each other suffer so much and not being able to make any of it better made us cry almost non-stop. When we looked at each other, we recognized that this was becoming a battle Callum's body was losing, and in our minds we were preparing ourselves for how many days or weeks we might have left with him. We didn't say this out loud, but we both knew it.

The next day Callum's condition wasn't any better. The hope that the ventilator would help his lungs and body recover a bit and improve his oxygen requirements hadn't turned into reality. The medications had done little to nothing to change his condition. The doctors still didn't know what was causing Callum's deterioration. The ICU team told us there was only one option left. It involved an oscillator, a special type of ventilator used only in very specific circumstances for patients with acute respiratory distress syndrome, known as ARDS. The oscillator pushes small volumes of oxygen in and out of the lungs at a very high frequency. In the struggle to support lungs damaged by ARDS, it's the last option.

One month before Callum was born, during my ICU rotation as a second-year resident physician, I cared for a patient who was on an oscillator. She was dying of end-stage liver disease and the ICU team was desperate to try anything that might help her. Sadly, she died two days after being admitted. I remembered that the oscillator ran continuously and was very loud. It sounded like a small freight train. It was upsetting to see it used then, and I was petrified to imagine what it would be like seeing Callum connected to it.

Callum would need to be anaesthetized and paralyzed with medications to prevent him from feeling discomfort and to allow the oscillator to operate as it needed to. In other words, he would be made unconscious while the machine completely took control of his breathing. Our ability to communicate with him would be non-existent. The team had no idea how long the oscillator would be used for. There were no certainties about anything. It could be many days and there might be no going back. Hours later, we blew Callum kisses as the nurse put him to sleep with IV medications. The respiratory therapist connected him to the oscillator and turned it on. Just as I remembered, it had a loud, low-frequency hum, like a train going by in the distance.

I walked to the window that looked over the street and began to cry. Trisha came over to comfort me. She could see in my face that I knew more about the oscillator than I had let on. She didn't ask, though. No words were needed. That night we just cried. We couldn't think or sleep or eat. All we could do was be there. I repeatedly stopped myself from thinking about Callum dying. I knew in the next few days I might be faced with contemplating living life without him, but we weren't there yet. We were on the precipice, for sure, but not beyond the point of no return. Instead I focused on what I could do for Trisha. How could I support her? What did she need? But I couldn't provide what she needed. All I could do was hold her, cry with her, and love her as much as I ever had. We were trapped together in this room with Callum, and Thai was with our family on the outside waiting for the three of us to come home and say it was okay.

I can't recall how long Callum was on the oscillator. I could be wrong, but I think three days passed with Trisha and me sitting beside his bed, reading books to him and spending a lot of time in relative silence. Occasionally, we visited with Thai and talked with family members in the hospital atrium or the ICU waiting room. I think I forced myself to eat a bit more and I tried very hard to smile for Thai and be interested in what he'd been doing with Nana and Papa and Grandpa Gene.

I made a trip to the copy centre across the street to print out colour pictures for Callum's room. I didn't care if parents didn't normally decorate their child's ICU room, especially if they were unconscious. Channelling what Judi had taught me the month before, I was determined that everybody who entered Callum's room would see him as a happy child and not an almost lifeless body connected to machines. This was selfish on my part, but I couldn't have cared less. I had no control over anything, but at the very least I could show the nurses, respiratory therapists, and physicians the handsome boy our Callum was.

During this time, the doctors told us his blood counts had improved and that he no longer required strict isolation precautions. The sixth and final stem cell transplant had done its job. Callum's immune system, although still weakened, was functioning properly. In previous cycles, this meant we could hold him and that he could have visitors and leave his room to play. But not this time. Everything was different. The joy we'd experienced on these days in previous cycles was absent. We couldn't hold him now that we were allowed to. Every part of Callum was connected by tubes to IV catheters, monitors, and other machines. He was unconscious, forced to lie flat on his bed, and his hands and feet were swollen with fluid. We couldn't hold even one hand. It was pure agony.

Back in September, when we arrived at Sick Kids for the last three cycles, we found out that Puppy couldn't sleep with Callum because of the isolation protocol. Our solution then was to put him in isolation too. Now that cycle six was completed and Callum's blood counts had improved, it was time for Puppy to come out of isolation. That was the deal we'd made. The problem was, Callum couldn't enjoy the moment. Regardless, I removed Puppy from the sterile bag and put him on the bed as a symbol. The other milestone that was supposed to happen was to add a charm to the bracelet Trisha had given Callum when he started chemotherapy. There were still two empty spots. One was for this very day – the end of chemotherapy and the return of normal blood counts. The other was for the day we were allowed to take him home.

Over the last month, before he needed oxygen, Callum and I had spent hours talking about those empty spots and which charms he would pick to fill them. We looked at the pros and cons of choosing a rainbow or a shining sun or a heart or a ladybug, and so on. I had bought at least half a dozen charms in anticipation of this day and I carried them with me, but there was no way I was putting one on if he couldn't share in the experience. Instead, I took the bracelet from his wrist and put it on mine. So that it would fit, I added all the charms I'd bought, but I left the two empty spots as they were. I wouldn't add to the bracelet without him, nor would I take it off. I would look after it until he was able to choose the charm he wanted.

Then one morning there was hope. The ICU staff saw that Callum's respiratory status had improved, his oxygen requirements had decreased, and some of his other blood work numbers were better. They thought it made sense for him to come off the oscillator and go back on a regular ventilator. It was good not only to hear that Callum's lungs were stronger, but that he would be allowed to wake up and we could communicate. It was the best day of a rough week. Over the next few hours, Callum's sedation was turned off, he was connected to the regular ventilator, and he started to wake up. Soon he tried to say hi to Trisha and me, despite the breathing tube in his throat and having been unconscious for three days. We were together again. Trisha and I felt total happiness to be able to enjoy Callum's company.

Our joy and hope were short-lived. No further progress was made and the reality of our situation hadn't changed. The specialists continued to be at a loss for what had caused Callum's deterioration, and he remained at constant risk of going back on the oscillator. The pediatric cardiologist came to do a bedside echocardiogram. I watched as he carefully and methodically used an ultrasound probe to see what was going on in Callum's heart and lungs. By assessing the heart chamber sizes and the speed, direction, and pressures of blood flow, it provided a lot of information about how they were functioning. I recognized that some of the measurements and pictures were grossly abnormal. Because of my training, and having had patient experiences in the pediatric ICU and pediatric cardiology, I knew what the consequences were when the cardiologist told us that Callum had developed severe pulmonary hypertension and a severely dilated cardiomyopathy. His opinion was that it was irreversible and was most likely due to chemotherapy-induced toxicity. With those words, I lost all hope of Callum ever living a fraction of the life he'd once had.

CHAPTER 8

The Last Days

Even if Callum survived this crisis, he would be at risk of sudden death almost every day for the rest of his life. It would be very unlikely that he would be able to run and jump and swim and play ever again. Even in the best-case scenario, if the damage was partially reversible, Callum would need a double heart and lung transplant in the next few years. But he was too small. A transplant wouldn't last long enough for a growing body. Or would it? Even if things happened perfectly, he would first have to qualify as a candidate for the transplant list and he would have to be lucky enough to receive a match during a small window of time. All of the what-ifs seemed to spiral out of control. Every possibility ended in more danger, uncertainty, and likely death from complications. None ended in the four of us going home to get better and play again.

That night, I couldn't shake the feeling of having no way out. If Callum lived, he would be crippled by what chemotherapy had done to his heart and lungs. He'd never regain his life as he knew it, not even close. But the alternative was not surviving. I couldn't bear to think of that. How could the three of us live without him? It was a reality that was inescapable. All I could do was cry. Every hour that I was awake now, I cried. Even when I slept, which was only a few hours at a time, I dreamed of Callum dying and cried in my dreams. My entire consciousness was consumed with agony and despair. When I looked at Trisha, I could see she was grieving just as I was, yet I could do nothing to help. I felt so inadequate and powerless. All I could do was be with Callum in his room, with Trisha beside us. I urgently needed to be present for every last moment the three of us had together.

I woke up early the next morning in a panic. I looked at Callum's oxygen requirements and spoke with the respiratory therapist who had worked overnight. I realized he needed to go back on the oscillator within the next few hours, which meant another medicated coma and being paralyzed again. I woke Trisha up and we called her mom at RMH. It was 6 a.m. and we told her that she and Thai needed to come immediately because Thai might not have another chance to talk to his brother before he died. If that's what was happening, we knew they needed to say goodbye to each other.

I met Nana and Thai at the front doors of Sick Kids. It was still dark and quiet outside. I walked them up to the ICU and snuck them into Callum's room. I didn't ask anyone for permission. According to official hospital policy, 6:15 a.m. wasn't an acceptable time for visiting, nor were children generally allowed in the ICU at all. If I got into trouble, so be it. What would they do to me, anyway? Was I wrong to think like that? I didn't care. I believed Thai's future without Callum depended on this moment. If Callum wasn't going to wake up, I'd never forgive myself if Thai hadn't seen him one last time.

Before entering Callum's room, I prepared Thai for what he was about to experience. To really see Callum and be present with him, he'd need to block out the machines, the monitors, the tube in Callum's throat, and his frail body. I told Thai that if he felt like crying, it was okay. What was happening was wrong and unfair and shocking, but real. It was an overwhelming experience for all of us when he walked into the room, but he did great and made us very proud. At four years old, he didn't seem to care about all the medical equipment. He saw his brother lying on his bed and simply said, "Hi Callum." Callum lifted his hand, waved at his big brother, and smiled. Trisha and I understood that this was goodbye. We didn't want to say it, but we knew. Before he or Callum realized how upsetting this was, I took Thai out into the hallway.

Callum was put back on the oscillator a few hours later. Trisha and I sobbed at his bedside as he was made unconscious again. Numerous times that morning, the nurses and physicians told us not to panic. There was time, they said, for things to improve. All was not lost. They told us to stay hopeful. I heard them, but their comments didn't penetrate my wall of grief. I understood why they were saying those words, but it didn't make sense. We were losing the battle. Callum was slipping away and the three of us, Trisha, Thai, and myself, would have to live without him.

The next few days were torture. Trisha and I continued to struggle. Callum's body was so frail and small, he was barely recognizable. His skin colour seemed artificial, and his hands and feet were full of fluid and triple their normal size. At times, the only part of his body we could hold was his left foot. We wept continuously. This was our time and we knew we had only a few days left. We knew it as a fact, even if no one else would admit it. Trisha and I became frail ourselves. We hardly ate or drank, and at night only slept for thirty-minute intervals. We became more nervous and irritable with the nurses and respiratory therapists. To everyone else in our life, we could only show despondence. Knowing we were in the final stretch, I often wondered what I would say to myself as a physician, brother, husband, and father. The stereotypical phrases, concerns, and suggestions seemed inconsequential.

I didn't care if I lost ten or twenty pounds or more by not eating. What did it matter if I was functioning on next to no sleep for days at a time? It didn't goddamn matter. This nightmare was only getting worse and soon enough, we would leave the hospital without Callum. I could eat better and try to sleep more in the weeks and months to come. Our physical suffering seemed insignificant compared to Callum's suffering.

Thinking back, Trisha, Callum, and I seemed interconnected like the gentle alien and the little boy were connected in the Steven Spielberg movie ET. As ET grew sicker in the movie, so did the boy, but their connection couldn't be explained. They were unified in spirit and body. As ET was dying, the boy's body was dying too. Our bodies weren't suffering like Callum's, but our hearts and souls were. Part of Trisha was dying as Callum was dying and the same was true of me.

The final days of Callum's life brought not just a mounting fear of his death, but of not being with him when he died. This made spending any time outside his ICU room horribly anxiety-provoking. We forced ourselves to leave for periods of fifteen minutes to see Thai and our family in the waiting room or to have a three-minute shower next to the ICU or to eat a chocolate bar from a vending machine. So many people came to the hospital. One by one, they tried to find a way to see us. Later we found out that some friends had come just to be close to us, knowing they likely wouldn't see us but not letting that deter them from being in the same building to share our grief.

The people who took the best care of us during that time were new friends we'd become close to at Sick Kids, particularly David (our social worker since the beginning), Annie (Dr. Huang), Ute (Dr. Bartels), and Zia (my classmate from medical school). They courageously found their way to Callum's room as regularly as they could. Their visits were important to us. They grieved for Trisha and me, and they grieved for Callum. They had met him before his illness became critical and had enjoyed his company and gap-toothed smile. They all cried with us, which helped immensely. Perhaps most importantly, they didn't try to make the situation less tragic than it was. They often stood with us in silence. I remember thinking that Annie and Ute were the kind of caring, compassionate, and imperfect doctors I aspired to be. They had run out of choices. They had ordered an aggressive chemotherapy regimen to try to cure Callum and something had gone horribly wrong. There they were standing with us saying they were sorry, yet Callum's cancer had never provided other options.

I remember sitting at Callum's bedside wondering how I would interact with patients and families when the end of life was near, being in that place now myself. I thought of how my career as an ER doctor and medical educator was forever altered. I thought of the humanity in caring for people and facing grief together. I knew then that surviving Callum's death and grieving my son would have a profound impact on my path as a doctor and teacher. Not knowing what lay ahead in my medical practice, I promised myself and Callum that I would choose to be brave. I would have courage to stand silently with families, to be present and vulnerable and not shy away from speaking the honest truth.

The evening before Callum died, I was afraid. I had accepted that he was about to die, but I couldn't imagine not having his presence. Even on the oscillator, paralyzed and sedated, he was there. He was alive and I could feel him, touch him, and be with him. I was afraid of what would come next. I went to the chapel next to the ICU and had a conversation with God. It was part prayer and part meditation.

Despite growing up Catholic and going to church every Sunday for most of my life, my relationship with God had evolved into respecting a spiritual higher power. I no longer blindly followed an all-knowing divinity, as had been taught to me by teachers, priests, and older family members. I had long ago relinquished the childish view that God could change things if you prayed hard enough. Instead of praying at church, I would often reflect on becoming a better person. I enjoyed those quiet times at Mass as I knelt there, even if I didn't always agree with what the priest was saying or the prayers being recited. I had learned to think of the bigger world, my place in it, and what I could do to improve myself.

In the chapel that day, I thought of everyone praying for us back home in Kingston. We had a strong community of support and hundreds of prayers were being made on our behalf. But more praying for a miracle didn't seem realistic or appropriate right now. It actually seemed dangerous for me to cling to a hope that would isolate me from reality. Instead, I asked God, Is there any way this path can be altered? I knelt in silence and knew the answer. Then I asked, If not, will You help me find the strength to not only survive, but to support Trisha and Thai in their suffering? I needed to know in my deepest self that I wouldn't falter as a husband and father. I couldn't let that happen – ever. In those final moments of kneeling in the chapel, I wasn't so much hoping for a miracle as I was trying to find the inner courage and strength to face what lay ahead. I was truly afraid, but my family needed me more than ever, and I was resolved in mind and spirit to do my best for them.

The last day of Callum's life came. All the signs were there. The blood tests showed worsening organ damage throughout his body. The medications being used to support his blood pressure were almost maxed out. The oxygen settings on the ventilator were nearly at 100 percent. Seeing all this, I asked Trisha shortly after we woke up if I could talk to her about what we would do when Callum's heart stopped and a Code Blue was called. More specifically, I was asking if she'd agree to tell the team not to call a Code Blue. When Callum's heart stopped, I wanted everything to stop. I didn't want the ICU team doing CPR on him, nor did I want them to "shock his heart" with a defibrillator. I told her it would be totally futile and I didn't want those images in my mind, or in her mind, for the rest of our lives. Trisha wasn't ready to talk about it. I suggested that we discuss it with the ICU team when we saw them at morning rounds.

A few hours later, the attending physician stopped by to see us. We hadn't met him before. He seemed nice and was more optimistic than I'd anticipated. He said it wasn't time to talk about a DNR (do not resuscitate) status and that Callum wasn't going to die today. He also told us that rather than stay cooped up in Callum's room, we needed to go out for at least an hour to spend time with Thai and our family. He very deliberately told us not to lose all hope. For once, we listened. His hopeful words had snapped me temporarily out of my depression. I decided to make plans to visit Thai at RMH for an hour that afternoon. I called and said that I missed him and was looking forward to being with him soon.

On my walk there, I actually stopped along the way to get something to eat. For ten minutes, I sat down and ate a salad, sandwich, and yogurt, and drank a smoothie. Afterwards, I felt stronger and less anxious. Those few minutes helped me pull myself together a bit. I continued on my way, knowing Thai was waiting. He was ecstatic to see me.

Back at the hospital, Trisha was having a better afternoon as well. She'd been blessed with an hour or two of quiet time with Callum, with minimal interruptions. She felt surprisingly calm and relaxed. She talked to Callum more than usual, even though he was unconscious and unresponsive. While I was gone, she read book after book to him, all his favourites, like Dora the Explorer, Blue's Clues, Magenta's New Glasses, 12 Little Ducklings, The Hungry Caterpillar, and more. As always, the simple act of reading to him brought Trisha a lot of joy. She did this without hesitation as the nurses and respiratory therapist moved around the room, carrying out their usual duties.

For a few minutes, while the nurse was charting in the adjacent room and the respiratory therapist had gone somewhere, Trisha was alone with Callum. During that brief moment, and for the first time, she gave him permission to die. She told him out loud that she knew it was time and she couldn't ask him to continue living like this. She couldn't ask him to stay alive for her anymore. It was time to say goodbye.

Over at Ronald McDonald House, Thai and I were playing on the floor in our room. He was proudly showing me how he'd arranged all the toy cars in rows and lines to depict city streets and a train station. For a few minutes, I was completely engaged and enjoying my time with him. I wasn't worried about not being at the hospital. Then my phone rang. It was Trisha. "You better come now," she said. "Callum's blood pressure is falling." I didn't let her finish. I gathered up Thai and the two of us hurried down the stairs to find Nana in the kitchen. I told her that I had to go and gave her a look that said this could be it. I told Thai, "Daddy has to go, honey. I'll see you in a little bit, okay? I love you."

I ran down the stairs and out the door. I could feel myself starting to panic. My heart was pounding as I raced across the street. I found myself on the sidewalk at the corner of

Yonge and Gerrard, waiting for a red light to turn green. The street was packed with cars and I was wondering if I should J-walk through the traffic when my phone rang again. This time Trisha was screaming, "Damon… Run! Run!" The front doors of the hospital were just a few blocks away. I ran into the traffic, then slowed slightly to maneuver between the moving cars. On the other side, I resumed my sprint, fully in the throes of fear and panic. I summoned all my physical strength, telling myself, I know I can make it, I know I can make it.

I covered the first two blocks, then the third. My heart, lungs, and legs began to burn. I had one more major intersection, then three blocks to the front doors. I easily crossed the intersection, ignoring the scores of people staring at this man who was running for everything he was worth. By the time I closed in on the final two blocks, my body was really suffering, but I was fuelled by desperation. No amount of physical pain would stop me. During the last few hundred metres, I started talking out loud to Callum. "Please wait for me, honey. Please. Please. I'll make it. Don't let the doctors stop. Come on, honey. Just give Daddy sixty seconds. I'm almost there with you. Not much longer. Please, honey. Let Daddy make it. I can't let you leave without me." Now tears were streaming down my face.

At the same time, images of our family life flashed through my mind: Callum's birth, Trisha breastfeeding at home, our trip to Disney World, the previous Christmas, our month in Boston during my training, lying in bed with my boys at night, Trisha in her wedding dress. So many pictures of happiness flooded my mind. It seemed like a movie, but it was real, happening right now, to me, to Trisha, to all of us. Our life was unravelling before our eyes.

I finally reached the hospital and ran through the doors and across the atrium, maintaining my frantic pace. I climbed to the second floor, sidestepped multiple children, parents, and doctors crowding the hallway, and reach the back entrance of the ICU. My breathing was out of control and I thought my body might collapse. I navigated my way to Callum's room, where a team of doctors, nurses, and respiratory therapists was performing CPR on my son.

Trisha was standing at the end of the bed. She was silent, with tears running down her face, but I could see that she was calm. We'd known for many days that this moment was inevitable. She reached out her hand and I grabbed it. I could tell she was relieved I'd made it in time. We shared a brief moment, maybe a few seconds, and then focused on Callum and the team. The monitors that had shown no heart rhythm or pulse were now telling us that both had returned. The team had stopped doing CPR. Callum was still alive. As tears poured out, I said to him, quietly, "Thank you, honey. Thank you for letting Daddy make it here. I'm here. Mommy's here. We're ready, honey. We know it's time."

Looking around the room, I took in the entire Code Blue team, the multiple staff, the crash cart, the look of intense effort on everyone's faces, and on Callum's chest, defibrillation pads. Everything confirmed Trisha's screams of just a few minutes ago. This was it. There was no doubt. We were losing Callum now.

Trisha and I approached the bed, needing to hold any part of his fragile body that wasn't connected to IVs, machines, and tubes. I held his right foot while Trisha had her hand on his abdomen and chest. We then watched Callum's heart rhythm on the monitor get slower and slower. We watched his blood pressure become so low it no longer registered. The team of doctors and nurses saw this too and prepared to restart the CPR and give powerful IV medications. Trisha and I looked at each other, then said, "Stop." We said it again, "Please stop."

At first, no one on the team heard us, maybe because they were concentrating so hard on Callum. Or maybe because our plea was barely audible. As the tears ran down my face, I stepped in front of the doctor in charge and tried again, more firmly this time. "Please stop." The whole team looked at Trisha, and then at me, to confirm what they thought they'd just heard. "Yes, we want you to stop. Please. Stop," I said. And they did. Then we watched Callum die.

He was gone and the world changed forever.

CHAPTER 9

He's Gone

We stood beside Callum's lifeless body, weeping and holding each other. It didn't feel real but there was no way to escape the reality. As soon as the nurses and physicians left the room and we were alone, I wanted all the tubes and monitors off of him. When that was done, one last time, we were able to hold him. Next to the bed was a rocking chair. We curled ourselves into it, with Trisha on top of me and Callum in her arms, while I held them both. We wept for a long time. A few people came and went but we barely noticed. We didn't want anyone – no staff, no minister or priest, no family or friends. All we wanted was to be present in those last minutes with Callum. We sat there embracing each other, wondering how our life was supposed to continue without him.

After a long while, I wanted to tell Trisha how much I loved her and how lucky the kids and I were to have her. Throughout the last six months, I'd watched her act selflessly and courageously. I thought of the many times during Callum's illness that she'd ignored the status quo in favour of choosing our own path. She didn't care what other people did, what was expected, or how things usually worked. Doing what was best for our children was her gospel, and everything flowed from there. Whether it was insisting on enrolling Thai in kindergarten next door to Sick Kids, figuring out how to spend twenty-four hours a day with Callum and Thai, expecting our children to behave appropriately, declining offers of assistance because they didn't suit our needs, or driving home the notion that "home is where we are" made me love her more than I ever thought possible.

Sitting and holding her, I wanted to tell her that she was everything to me and the kids. As I tried to catch my breath so I could speak, through her own tears she said, "Callum, Thai, and I are lucky to have you … you're a great father … and we love you." If I hadn't loved her enough already, there she was worrying about me even as I was worrying about her. In that moment, holding Callum for the last time, we were completely connected in our thoughts, emotions, and actions. No one would ever understand that moment or those months of struggle except us. I was comforted by this thought. I knew I would always look after Trisha and that she would always look after me.

Minutes later, we acknowledged there would never be a time that felt right to let go of Callum and leave, but we had to. Thai was waiting for us outside with our parents and we had to let them know that Callum had died. When the offer was made to make an imprint of his foot in plaster, we gave the nurse his body and said our final goodbyes to our baby.

After leaving the room, Trisha and I stopped in the hallway. Before meeting everyone in the waiting room, we needed a few minutes to check in with each other about what would happen next and in the coming days. We wanted control over the things that were most important to us. We'd had many days and nights in the ICU to consider life without Callum and what this moment would look like. We hadn't discussed it, but I was certain we had the same thoughts.

I said that I wanted to be the one to tell Thai that Callum had died, and I asked Trisha if she would tell our parents. We then agreed on Callum's funeral arrangements. Neither of us wanted to bury his body in a cemetery. Instead, we would spread his ashes in our special family places at a later date. We would ask the City of Kingston for permission to plant a tree in the park where we'd had Callum's early third birthday party at the beginning of September. We would also ask them if we could place a stone bench in the little waterfront park across the street from Nana and Papa's house where the kids had spent many happy hours together. We imagined going to these places for years to come, to think and cry and be together, and to laugh and play.

Everything we did had to make sense and have meaning. It was of the utmost importance to us that our plans for remembering and celebrating Callum's life needed to be more than going through the motions because we didn't have the energy to decide what we actually wanted. There was no way we would leave it up to others to guess what was best for us because we were in too much pain to make the choices ourselves.

Holding hands, we walked towards the waiting room. I watched Thai come to greet me. It was around 6 p.m. on a Sunday. The hospital was quiet and dark. I remember thinking it was important to use "died" so that Thai's four-year-old brain could start processing the magnitude of its meaning. In front of the elevators, I bent down and said, "Honey, Callum died. The medicine didn't make him better. He couldn't get better. He's gone to Heaven … he's gone forever, honey. Do you know what that means?"

Thai looked at me as tears fell down my face. He said, "Does that mean Callum is happy again, he's feeling good again? Is he better in Heaven, Daddy?" "Yes, he is, honey," I answered. "Do you know what it means to die and be in Heaven, sweetie?" Thai explained, as only a small child can, that it meant Callum was gone and we wouldn't see him again, or at least not until we died when we were old. He asked if Nanny Turner (Trisha's grandmother, who had passed away earlier that year) would be in Heaven with him. When I told him yes, he replied, "Okay." I said we were returning home the next day and that we would all be sad because we'd miss Callum so much. Again Thai asked, "But he's not having any pain, right Daddy? He's happy and healthy again in Heaven? He's better, right Daddy"? "Yes, honey, he is. Let's go give Mommy a hug. She misses you."

The next hours were a blur. We cried with our parents and we cried on the phone telling our siblings. We all cried with each other. I remember thinking that I didn't know how we would leave the hospital without Callum. I don't remember the moment we left Sick Kids or walking with our family back to Ronald McDonald House. I wouldn't call my condition shock. Rather, those details were so inconsequential that I didn't pay attention to them. My mind was focused on Callum and Trisha and Thai. Back in our room, I faintly recall a few moments with family, but most of the evening is fuzzy. Finally, Trisha, Thai, and I climbed into bed together. Still crying, I held onto Thai and tried to close my eyes. I knew I needed to sleep but I wasn't sure how that would happen. Eventually, extreme fatigue took over and Trisha and I slept for a few hours.

Waking up the next morning, my heart and mind knew Callum was gone. Sleep had changed nothing. It was time to go home. One by one, family members arrived to comfort us and help us pack up our things. The specifics of that morning aren't clear. I remember Trisha and me telling our parents about our plans for Callum's cremation and funeral, and about his stone bench and the tree. We would need their help. I called the funeral home director and the priest who married us, Monsignor Lynch. They agreed to meet us the next day to talk about Callum's visitations and funeral. I wrote a brief email to friends and colleagues to say that Callum was gone. "Trisha and I are heartbroken to tell you…" is how it started. With those words, almost everyone in our lives found out that Callum had died and we were coming home. I couldn't bear telling anyone else in person.

Leaving the cocoon where we'd lived apart from the rest of the world was a gut-wrenching experience. During the almost six months I'd sat in the hospital, and especially during the last two weeks in the ICU, I hadn't envisioned the uniquely tragic moment of leaving Toronto without Callum. Except for the three times he'd had surgery or procedures under anaesthesia, Callum had never been without Trisha or me for more than ten minutes. Now we were forced to leave without him forever.

My father-in-law was in charge of driving us home. I was a passenger in my own car for the first time. Everything felt wrong. Trisha and Thai sat in the back beside Callum's empty car seat. I felt a crushing emptiness. I vividly remember driving out of Toronto on November 12, 2006, sixteen hours after Callum died. It was late morning on a cloudy, cold fall day. I wept silently as we turned onto the Don Valley Parkway, the skyline of downtown Toronto in the background. We were soon on the 401 heading east. I cried for the entire three-hour drive.

I arrived home in a fog. Our house felt empty with only the three of us in it. My sense of hollowness was even worse than I'd feared. I longed to be back at Sick Kids. My body ached in a way that made me want to scream until I couldn't scream anymore. There was a desire in me to destroy everything in my path until my hands and feet were shattered. I welcomed the thought of suffering. I wanted to embrace a physical pain that matched my mental anguish. It's hard to describe what it felt like to lose Callum. Think of an internal abyss that's deeper and darker than anything you can imagine. I felt like throwing up all the time. I wanted to howl. The pain penetrated every fibre of my being. It didn't seem possible that I could carry on living with that level of pain.

To make matters worse, it was like we were trapped in our own home. Every possession was a reminder that Callum was gone. Our family pictures on the walls, the photo albums on the shelves, the bath toys and screensaver, Callum's tricycle in the garage, the wagon, his closet full of clothes, his empty room, and on and on. Even the sounds in our house were different, and it seemed they always would be. There was no music or laughter in the background. Thai played quietly by himself. The house was often silent except for the sounds of Trisha and me crying.

That first night, the quiet and darkness were horrible. I didn't know how I would endure it. But it was only the beginning. I soon learned that nighttime hours were more brutal than daytime. Alone with my emotions, drained from the day's struggle to keep myself together, without the benefit of sunlight and with no activities to hide behind, the darkness brought out my worst fears and rachetted up my anguish. It was nearly impossible to fall asleep. I couldn't image being more exhausted, but my mind wouldn't stop flashing on memories – of running to the hospital, waiting during surgery, leaving Sick Kids for the last time, holding Callum's lifeless body, Trisha weeping, Thai waking up in the middle of the night and crying, Callum playing at Disney World, the boys sleeping together, Callum's first birthday, Christmas last year….

On waking up in the morning, I had to force myself to think that my next move was to get out of bed. I had to function, at least on a basic level. Even though I didn't want to move or think or care about anything, that wasn't an option. I needed to shower, get dressed, eat something, and encourage Trisha and Thai to do the same. It seemed like those simple tasks should be doable compared to what lay ahead of us that day – meetings with the funeral home director and Monsignor Lynch to plan Callum's visitations and funeral. Sitting in their offices felt surreal. They were very compassionate and helpful, and they guided us along gently. We told them we wanted to do things our way and they agreed, for which we were very thankful. Monsignor Lynch, who was no longer at the cathedral where Trisha and I were married, which was where we wanted to have the service, said he would arrange it. Returning home, we were relieved to have those meetings over with. We had survived the first part.

Nearing twenty-four hours at home, the phone started ringing. Family and friends were checking in with us. There were offers of food, tea, and companionship, and did we want someone to pick up groceries or watch Thai for a few hours? People offered anything they could think of. Often the best offers were just talking and listening on the phone. Knowing people are thinking about you, worried about you, and grieving for you helps so much. Having a community of support is more important than just about anything.

Beyond phone calls and talking to family, I don't remember much of those first two days except feeling totally overwhelmed, and even more so after everyone was in bed. On the second night, the house quiet, I sat on the couch and stared out the window at the blackness of the sky. The reality of what was happening started to sink in on a deeper level. This was my new life, our new normal. For the first time ever, I couldn't see my path into the future. Somewhere around 3 a.m., I finally fell asleep. In my dreams I saw Callum playing and I reached out for him and he hugged me. I started to cry. My consciousness was present enough to recognize that I was dreaming and know the hug wasn't real.

Waking up that morning, I remembered my dream and was overcome with emotion. Not wanting to upset Trisha, who was still asleep, I got up and went into Callum's room. Everything was just as we'd left it at the end of summer – his IV pole and kangaroo infusion pump for his gastric tube, the nutritional formula on the dresser, toys on the floor, his bed, his clothes, the pictures on the walls. Knowing I shouldn't, I lay down on his bed anyway. I thought to myself, This isn't good. You need to get up. Get up! You can't start this routine. It isn't healthy. Get up. But I couldn't will myself to do it. I stayed on Callum's bed for several minutes, until Thai came and stood in the doorway. He looked at me with confusion and fear, and then he walked away. I jumped up and cursed myself for letting him see me like that.

Minutes later, the IV pole, kangaroo pump, nutritional formula, pictures, and Callum's bed were in the garage. Trisha and I tidied up Callum's clothing and toys and sat down with Thai to tell him we'd decided to make Callum's room a special place to play in. We talked about what we should put there and said we'd go shopping together later that day to pick out new furniture and decorations. We came home with a comfy chair, a blanket box to hold all our favourite memories of Callum, and a bright, colourful painting for the wall.

In the moment when Thai saw me lying on Callum's bed, I realized we needed to learn how to talk together about being lonely and missing Callum. We couldn't have Thai watching Trisha and me cry and feeling distant from us. Not only was it good to do something creative, constructive, and proactive to help us move forward as a family, like make Callum's room into a special playroom, Trisha and I needed to be conscious of how the three of us could grieve together. From that day on, we talked about helping Thai grieve with us in a safe and developmentally appropriate way, and we considered how our actions and decisions affected him and his grieving process. It was important that he see us cry, laugh, work hard, and love each other, and that he be able to do the same.

After arranging the new furniture in Callum's room, we looked around and picked out our favourite things that reminded us of Callum. We placed them in the blanket box until it was full. Inside the box were toys, clothes, pictures, books, puppets, stuffed animals, and the plaster imprint of Callum's foot from the day he died. We hung the new painting on the wall. We brought toys from Thai's room and the play area downstairs and put the computer on the shelf along with all the DVDs. We sat together on the new chair, which we'd placed in the corner, and we talked about other ways we could use the room. Before I knew it, Thai was playing cars and trains on the floor and I was sitting in the chair watching him. Trisha came to sit on my lap and we felt relieved that we'd accomplished something.

CHAPTER 10

Callum's Goodbye Party

Two days after Callum died, his obituary, written by my dad, appeared in our local newspaper. With it was a photo of Callum smiling at Disney World, taken just two weeks before he was diagnosed with cancer.

DAGNONE, CALLUM GENE (TURNER)
October 24, 2003 – November 11, 2006

Best friend of Thai. Inspiration always to his mother Trisha and father Damon. Joyful grandchild to Don and Sheila, Linda, Gene and Danielle. Wondrous free spirit to his Aunts: Tracey (David), Tiffany (Sean), Marla and Uncles: Joel (Nancy) and Vico (Heather). Eager playmate for Jacob, Turner, Claire, Sam, Ella, Ethan and Cole. Loyal companion of Banff. Your smile opened the door to our hearts. Your laughter and giggles infused our veins. Your bravery strengthened us in our goodbye. The harvest moon, the spring flowers, the summer rainbows and the winter snow angels will be your constant blessing upon us.

Friends will be received at the Township Chapel of Gordon F Tompkins Funeral Homes, 435 Davis Drive (Taylor Kidd Blvd at Centennial Drive) on Tuesday, November 14 from 7-9 p.m and Wednesday November 15 from 2-4 and 7-9 p.m. Mass of Christian Burial will be held in St. Mary's Cathedral, on Thursday, November 16, 2006 at 10:30 a.m. A reception to follow at Nana and Papa Turner's home, for family and close friends. Please direct your donations to the Ronald McDonald House or the Canadian Cancer Society in Callum's memory.

Reading Callum's obituary was crushing for me and confirmed what I feared in my heart – that I would never be the happy-go-lucky Damon again, and Trisha would never be the eternally optimistic, content Trisha. These thoughts could have left me in a trance all day, but today was the visitation at the funeral home. We had to greet the world without Callum and there were a lot of uncertainties. What would people say? Would they try to be positive? How would they react to us? Would they be able to just be with us and share in our grief? Would they cry with us and offer the companionship of their simple presence? I hoped so.

How many times in my life had I heard "What doesn't kill you only makes you stronger" and "You're only given what you can handle" and "You're a better person for going through this struggle"? I prayed no one would say those words this week. I didn't know if I could take it. Those sayings made the person speaking them feel better by protecting their minds from the reality of someone else's tragedy, loss, and grief. Also, they're just not true, at least, not on our scale. Trisha, Thai, and I weren't stronger. We were given far too much to handle. And we weren't better people. We were weaker, sadder, angrier, and more vulnerable. This wasn't pessimism talking. This was knowing we'd been broken and the pieces would never come together to make us whole again, because Callum wasn't coming back. When a huge part of me was being a parent, loving the process of nurturing our children with Trisha, how could losing Callum not crush me forever? Moving forward right now was defined by getting through the next few days. I'd worry about the rest of my life later.

I still remember the first person, outside of family and immediate friends, I told that Callum had died. It happened in Starbucks while waiting in line for my coffee. One of the grandparents we knew from Thai's daycare heard my name called. He came over to ask how Callum was doing and to let me know that the entire daycare was thinking about us. Was Callum home? How were things going? He reminded me of how much fun the kids had had the last time they played together. I stood there listening, wondering how to tell him. I needed a few moments to prepare. I wasn't worried about myself, I was only worried about him. He was smiling and so happy. I knew I was about to devastate him and there was no escaping it.

"Callum died two days ago, on Sunday. We just came home," I said. He struggled to say something but he was speechless. I could see how heartbroken he was and I recognized immediately my desire to comfort him, to protect him from the shock, but I knew that was impossible. I put my hand on his hand as tears welled up in our eyes. We just looked at each other as he tried to say how sorry he was. I saw him crying in the parking lot as he was leaving. Somehow his tears helped me a little.

A couple of hours later, we arrived at the funeral home to go over a few last details and get our bearings before everyone arrived. The director wanted to make sure the flower arrangements were perfectly placed and the collages of pictures were displayed in the right spots. He told us where we would stand and where the visitors would be ushered into the room. He also said we had to confirm that it was Callum's body in the coffin, which was closed. He mentioned it had something to do with rules and the certificate of death. I wasn't ready for this surprise. Trisha and I had said our goodbyes on Sunday in the ICU and I didn't want to see my baby embalmed in a coffin.

After realizing that Trisha was equally terrified to look inside the coffin, I took a deep breath and very quickly confirmed that the body was his. Even though I'd barely looked in, seeing Callum like that was horrible and haunting. I immediately went over to the dozens of pictures on the poster boards. I needed to erase the image of his lifeless body in the coffin. Trisha came and held onto me as tears flowed down my face. We then went to our assigned places and waited for people to arrive.

Our family had come early and we talked together while waiting. It felt nice to be surrounded by people who were also struggling, grieving, and vulnerable. Soon Trisha and I felt more confident than we'd expected to, and we knew we could embrace what was about to unfold. As heartbroken as we were, we knew nothing would ever be as hard as watching Callum die. Nothing could compare to the anguish of holding him one last time in the rocking chair, then walking away for good. Today would be hard for sure, but it was also an opportunity to be with people who cared about us. We'd been isolated for so long, finally we could reconnect with our family, friends, and anyone else who wanted to see us that day.

Over the course of the evening, we grieved with a lot of people. What gave me the most comfort was having Trisha at my side and watching her interact with everyone. She was as graceful and genuine as I'd ever seen her. She was strong and composed, while still being vulnerable and open to whoever approached us. She held my hand and made sure I was okay. She made me proud to be her husband as we cried with and hugged the people who broke down in front of us.

Whether it was our friends from university, our teenage neighbour, friends of our parents, rarely seen relatives, colleagues from work, or old friends we hadn't talked to in a long time, everyone had an effect on us. We were especially comforted when close family friends, who in most situations were well composed, burst into tears with us. Somehow seeing them hurt so much on our behalf eased our pain a little. Having people share our suffering reaffirmed the deep connections we felt with them. It was like love magnified 100 times. Every visitor added to the safety net. These were the people who would look out for us, protect us, and nurture us as we tried to find our way back to life. We had a long way to go to reenter the world and we needed all the support and understanding they could give.

We had one conversation with an older couple that I think about often. They had been friends with my parents many years ago, when they were all first married and lived in the same apartment complex. They had come to tell us their story and offer comfort and advice. They lost their son almost thirty years ago. He was five when he died. They were devastated and remained so to that day. They said, "Don't let anyone tell you how to grieve for Callum. No one understands unless they've lost a child. We understand. We've survived because we looked after each other, and you and Trisha need to do the same. Be brave enough to find joy again, and be honest enough to accept the sorrow and pain you'll have for the rest of your life. It's been thirty years for us and it's still there."

In the few minutes they spent with us, they covered a lot of ground. They gave us permission to grieve and told us to support each other first and foremost. They reminded us that we needed to be brave for Thai, and we must embrace the joy that would come into our life. In their thirty years without their son, they lived every day with his memory front and centre in their minds. Instead of making us feel worse, their words were inspiring. They were real and honest. There was no sugar-coating the situation we were in. They told us we could manage if we were committed to each other and to trying.

My recollections of the next day are cloudy, but I remember talking with Trisha, when we were driving home from the last visitation, about how to prepare Thai for Callum's funeral the next day. He'd been with us the whole way and we'd involved him as much as a four-year-old could be involved. We'd explained what the coffin was, why people sent flowers, that lots of people would come to see us, and that the pictures of Callum and our family were an opportunity to show them how happy and special our family was. Thai had seemed to understand. At all three visitations, he'd played with his cousins and Aunt Kim,

Trisha's best friend from university, while we talked and cried with everyone who approached us. Now we didn't know what to say about the funeral.

We decided that Trisha would explain we were having a goodbye party for Callum. We'd get dressed up, go to church in a big fancy car, have Mass with our family and lots of friends, and then we'd go to Nana and Papa's for the last part of the party. There would be balloons, food, his cousins, his aunts and uncles and grandparents, and plenty of treats. We told him the day would be spent sharing stories of our favourite memories of Callum and all the fun we'd had together. Thai seemed to accept this without much difficulty.

Waking up on the morning of the funeral felt as agonizing as our first morning at home without Callum. It was dark and gloomy and cold outside, which matched our feelings inside. As much as I wanted to scream and cry and refuse to do anything at all, we had an agenda to carry out. Before the funeral, we were meeting our family at Trisha's parents' house. We needed to get moving so we could put this day behind us. When we arrived, all the people we cared about most were there: our parents, our siblings, and friends of the family. Everyone was busy preparing food and setting up tables for the reception that would follow the funeral. All I could think about was being in the exact same place, with all the same people, the day after Trisha and I were married. We were having a party to open wedding gifts. We felt celebratory and tremendously happy. Almost eight years later, we were immersed in tragedy.

Eventually, everyone got into their cars to go to the funeral. I braced myself for the next ninety minutes. Thai had never been in a limousine before and was excited to leave for Callum's goodbye party. Somehow, this made things even more painful. Trisha and I looked at each other, wondering how we'd get through it. My mind wandered as we drove away. We were headed to the same cathedral where Trisha and I were married and where our children were baptized. Monsignor Lynch was waiting for us there. He'd been with us at every major event in our life.

Inside the cathedral, we walked down the long aisle behind Callum's coffin. Our family followed behind us. We sat down in the pews at the front and the service started. Trisha was on my left, Thai on my right. I could see the part of the altar where we'd all stood together for Callum's baptism just three years before. Growing up, I'd been to the funerals of friends who died in tragic circumstances – meningitis, cancer, car accidents – and I always wondered how their parents suffered through their child's funeral, and even harder, continued living. Seeing them in the front pews, I tried to imagine how they would live their lives from that day on. Now I was in their place being watched by everyone, who no doubt were wondering how Trisha and I would move forward.

Knowing our memories of Callum's funeral would live with us forever, we'd asked for as much control over the service as Monsignor Lynch would allow. We talked with him about what he might say during the homily and carefully chose the music and readings, as well as who would read. Now the Mass was starting. Music played as Monsignor Lynch greeted the hundreds of people who had gathered. Thai listened intently while Trisha looked at me with the same anguish on her face as I knew was on mine. This was as real and tragic as life could be. Time literally stood still. Every event since Callum's death had seemed forced, out of order, and wrong, and today was no different. But we were surrounded by a community of family and friends who had come to pray and grieve together. This wasn't lost on me. I was grateful to have this church full of people who wished to share this moment with us.

Partway through the service, two teenage girls – sisters Nicole and Danielle – walked up to the altar to do a reading. They were our babysitters and had a special bond with our boys. Standing there in front of such a large crowd, they gathered their strength and began their reading. Watching them hesitate, then struggle, and finaly persevere, I was immensely proud of them. They read a poem called "The Little Blue Engine" written by one of our favourite children's authors, Shel Silverstein. It goes like this…

"The Little Blue Engine" - *Shel Silverstein*

The little blue engine looked up at the hill.
His light was weak, his whistle was shrill.
He was tired and small, and the hill was tall,
And his face blushed red as he softly said,
"I think I can, I think I can, I think I can."

So he started up with a chug and a strain,
And he puffed and pulled with might and main.
And slowly he climbed, a foot at a time,
And his engine coughed as he whispered soft,
"I think I can, I think I can, I think I can."

With a squeak and a creak and a toot and a sigh,
With an extra hope and an extra try,
He would not stop — now he neared the top —
And strong and proud he cried out loud,
"I think I can, I think I can, I think I can!"

He was almost there, when — CRASH! SMASH! BASH!
He slid down and mashed into engine hash
On the rocks below... which goes to show
If the track is tough and the hill is rough,
THINKING you can just ain't enough!

This poem, more than any other, summed up our journey. We'd tried so hard. Callum had tried so hard. We'd kept our chins up but we just didn't make it. It had all come crashing down.

During the homily, Monsignor Lynch said a few words about Callum, life, God, and the search for meaning. He talked about innocence, happiness, love, family, and struggle. I don't remember the details, only that he spoke in a way that captured Callum's essence and our love of parenting. The most important and poignant thing he said was, "Do not try to find meaning in Callum's death. There is no sense to be made from this loss. There is no higher meaning for what's happened. Why an innocent child would be robbed of his life and his parents robbed of the chance to raise their child is a mystery. It is wrong. Trisha and Damon and Thai are forever changed, and they will need your support to help them move forward." Sitting there, I wanted to thank him for being brave enough to speak the truth.

Soon after that it was time to leave. Walking down the aisle, I noticed everyone looking at me, but I was happy about it. So many people had come to support us. I felt lucky to be surrounded by all these caring friends and colleagues. I knew I was going to need every single one of them to find my way back to living. Seated in the limousine, we watched the crowd spill out the cathedral doors. We saw a lot of people we hadn't seen in many years. They had showed up first to the visitations and now to the funeral. On the way home, we reminded Thai that lots of people would be at Nana and Papa's house for the goodbye party. They were coming to celebrate Callum's life with us. Thai was happy. He wanted a big party for Callum, and it was about to happen.

As planned, Nana and Papa's house was overrun. Just like at our wedding party eight years before, family and friends were everywhere and they all wanted to spend a few minutes with us. It felt good to see everyone, cry with them, and receive hug after hug after hug. I still have clear memories of many of those people hugging me and holding me tight. The most unexpected and special visitors that day were Thai's JK teacher and principal from Orde Street Public School in Toronto. They were so out of place among our friends and family, standing there next to the fridge, waiting patiently to talk to us and particularly to Thai. They brought his artwork and school folder from the two months he'd spent there. They expressed their sincere condolences and told us what a special child Thai was, and that they'd been privileged to have him at their school.

During the party, Trisha and I used every last ounce of energy and emotion we had to cry, tell stories, and reminisce. I recall seeing my brothers, my sister Marla, my parents, Trisha's parents, and her sisters Tracey and Tiffany, all look at us with heavy hearts. I could see how worried they were. Their worry didn't go unappreciated, but there was nothing they could do beyond physically being there with us, engaging in conversation with our friends, and helping clean up after everyone went home.

For hours, a slideshow played on Papa's big-screen TV. It consisted of clips from our home videos and was put together by our brother-in-law Dave. It beautifully represented many of the small, precious moments we'd shared with our boys. We watched Callum at Disney World, running around, riding in a teacup, playing Hide-and-Seek with Thai at the hotel, jumping in the pool, and trying to lure ducks to our patio with cheesies. Minutes later, he was excited to see what Santa had brought for Christmas the previous year. And there he was playing with his new train set at Nana and Papa's, and wearing a scary mask and shouting BOO to surprise his brother. We saw images of the boys sleeping in bed peacefully. All these pictures prompted memories that flooded Trisha and me with emotion. It was overwhelming. Hearing Callum's voice and laughter, and watching his interactions with Thai, felt like raw agony and despair.

After the guests left, Trisha, Thai, and I crossed the street to the little lakeside park where he and Callum and his cousins had fed the ducks and thrown stones in the water many times. We told Thai that this was where we'd make a special spot to remember Callum. We told him about the stone bench with Callum's name on it and that it would be there forever. Whenever we wanted, we would come here to think about Callum, have chats with him in Heaven, enjoy picnics, and plant flowers. Going to a cemetery had no meaning for us. Instead, we wanted to scatter Callum's ashes in special places, where later we could go and find comfort. This made sense to us, and Thai seemed to like our ideas.

Standing in the park where Callum's bench would go, the three of us released the helium balloons from the party into the air. We told Thai they were going up to Callum in Heaven. He was excited by that and enjoyed watching them drift up and over the lake until they disappeared. The metaphor of the balloons drifting further and further away created an ache in my heart I can still feel today. I wanted to scream so loud. In that moment, I felt the same pain rush through me that I'd felt just days before, holding Callum's lifeless body. Watching those balloons rise up and disappear, I ached so badly for him. But I didn't scream. It would have frightened Thai and I couldn't have that. The goodbye party had been more for Thai than anyone else.

Finally, the day came to an end. Lying in bed, I couldn't sleep. Too many images, conversations, and memories were coursing through my mind, from that day and everything that had happened in the last week. Callum was gone. We were home. The wake and funeral were behind us. Now the three of us were alone. I accepted that we were forever damaged and broken. I thought of the balloons. I wondered what loving God would allow this amount of pain. I thought of Monsignor Lynch's words at the funeral and felt relief to know that he couldn't make sense of this tragedy either.

CHAPTER 11

Moving Forward

In the first week after the funeral, we were weaker, angrier, and lonelier than ever before. We knew we needed help, and though we had the support of family and friends, we needed more, someone with expertise who would be honest with us. Walking into our family doctor's office the week after Callum died was the start of a conscious effort by Trisha and me to open up about the most agonizing emotions we were dealing with. We talked about fear, anger, sadness, anxiety, guilt, rage, love, desire, failure, success and anything and everything that came to our minds. This was a safe place for us to express ourselves. The doctor listened while we did most of the talking.

Over the course of those first few visits, it was very hard to describe how much we hurt. We told our doctor it was especially difficult to tell our family the whole truth. It made almost everyone in our life cry when we spoke about our agony. It's not easy telling people that every day is a nightmare. The few times I said those words to the people closest to me, it brought them instantly to tears. We felt like it was too much for people to hear the truth about our pain and anguish.

I don't think the words we used were the hardest part. The deeper impact came from our delivery. The doctor could easily see the suffering and pain in my eyes, facial expressions, and body language. She observed my twitching, poor eye contact, and constant effort to hold back tears and sobs. She heard my voice cracking, stuttering speech, and uncharacteristic soft tone as I slowly tried to get my feelings out. But I knew I didn't need to worry in the same way about hurting her. It was her responsibility, as our family doctor, to care for us not as a friend, but as a clinician. In her expert role, she would listen to and advise us professionally. As a physician who had counselled many patients myself, I understood and appreciated her role.

I remember telling her on the third or fourth visit that I wanted to put my fist again and again through walls. I wanted to kick everything in my path, not to break it necessarily, but to feel physical pain as a way of releasing emotion. But I also felt impulses to break my bones and feel terrible pain in my body in the hope of distracting my mind. Trisha felt something similar. She talked about wanting to ram the car against another car or any object in her path. She was so consumed with rage at times, but had no outlet for it. At the end of our visits, after articulating these deep truths, I always felt a bit better. Our doctor's words of encouragement were helpful and I liked that she said we were brave and lucky to have each other.

During this time, we experienced many cherished moments with people close to us. Friends sent thoughtful letters, cards, poems, and stories. Sometimes the best thing was to get an unexpected email that simply said, "I'm thinking about you." I remember reading a poem late one night that our friend Cathy sent us. Since it was about grieving dads, written by an anonymous author, she meant it specifically for me. I've kept it close by ever since.

To Be a Man in Grief

> To be a man in grief,
> Since "men don't cry" and "men are strong,"
> No tears can bring relief.
>
> It must be very difficult to stand up to the test
> and field calls and visitors so she can get some rest.
>
> They always ask if she's alright and what she's going through,
> But seldom take his hand and ask, "My friend, but how are you"?

He hears her crying in the night and thinks his heart will break.

He dries her tears and comforts her, but "stays strong" for her sake.

It must be very difficult to start each day anew

And try to be so very brave. He lost his child too.

I read this poem at night when I was feeling sorry for myself, which was often. Sometimes I did feel like a bodyguard for Trisha, that my job was to be brave and strong and to protect her from the outside world. But I never felt isolated or unable to be vulnerable. It was nice, though, to read something written specifically for a father.

An important rule Trisha and I made early on was to never apologize for the many ways what had happened to us was affecting the rest of our lives. We never promised each other to be better or stronger or to cry less. I remembered all those times I sat in the hallways of Sick Kids or in the chair next to Callum's bed watching him sleep, wondering how we could ever survive or be the same. Now here we were. In those first days, I vowed to Trisha and to myself that I'd never say it was time to stop crying. Not ever.

If grief and bereavement were defined only by crying and sadness, it would be easier to manage. During those first weeks at home, Trisha felt physically unwell. She vomited every time she ate. The heartburn that had started while Callum was in hospital grew a lot worse. She could barely tolerate herbal tea, soup, and plain bread. Her already petite body had wasted away to nothing. She knew she'd lost too much weight, but despite her best efforts, she wasn't having any success at regaining it.

Seeing Trisha suffer was very hard, but watching Thai suffer was worse. His pain was quieter, lonelier, and more withdrawn. Thai's shy and reflective personality made it difficult for him to come out of his shell and for us to help him. Unlike other tragedies in life, we didn't have to explain to him what had happened. He'd been there every step of the way –

with us in the hospital and at Ronald McDonald House, and witnessing Callum grow weaker and die in those final weeks. Thai knew Callum was gone and did his best to accept our situation, as much as any four-year-old can. He loved his brother more than anyone else in the world, and his heart was as broken as ours.

With his brother gone, Thai played quietly by himself. Other than family, he didn't have any desire to interact with his friends. Even when Trisha and I played with him, read books to him, and did everything we could to help him, we could see how lonely and sad he was. We realized the best thing we could do was encourage him to tell us how he felt. We knew a lot was going on in his mind, and if we could get him to tell us about it, we could help him navigate his emotions and memories and figure out how to view the world.

One of the strategies we used was to touch base with Thai every night during his bedtime routine. Just like before, we lay beside him in bed and read stories. But now we focused more on his feelings and thoughts. We asked him if anything nice had happened during the day and waited for his reply. We asked about any sad or lonely times he'd experienced, then waited. We talked about favourite memories we had of Callum and what made them so special. Just before it was time to turn out the light, we asked if there was anything else he'd like to talk about. Sometimes there was, but often not.

A few weeks after we were home, Thai told us something unexpected during one of those bedtime talks. He said he was upset that he hadn't been in the ICU with Trisha and me when Callum died, and that the doctors and nurses got to watch Callum go to Heaven, but he didn't. He told us how unfair it was that he didn't get to say goodbye. He was angry that the doctors and nurses were there, but he wasn't. He cried telling us this. It had been on his mind for some time and now he was letting it out.

That night, we talked for a long time about Heaven, the difference between Callum's soul and his body, Callum's unconscious state during the last days of his life, and even spirituality and eternity. We started by telling him that he did get to say goodbye to his brother, even before the doctors did. We reminded him of Nana bringing him from RMH early in the morning a few days before Callum died to have a last visit with him while he was still awake. We told Thai that the moment he and Callum waved at each other was their goodbye. When the doctors and nurses were in the room on the last day, it wasn't special like it was when Thai had been there and Callum was conscious. He thought about everything we said, asked a few more questions, and eventually said he felt better. He was asleep a few minutes later.

Right away, Trisha and I sat down on the couch and talked about how we could encourage more conversations like this. What else could Thai be thinking? We needed to help him develop a better understanding of Heaven, spirituality, life, and death, and why sometimes unexpected, unfair, and tragic events happened. We wanted him to know that despite his sadness, he could find peace and joy and happiness in life, just as we'd had before, when it was the four of us. We realized he needed images of Heaven he could store in his mind that would help him make sense of his memories and emotions. We couldn't take it for granted that he knew what Heaven was. Our job was to give it structure so he could imagine where Callum's soul had gone.

This was a daunting task, but Trisha and I were confident we were the only ones who could do it. Thai had been at our side throughout Callum's illness, when we'd been comfortable teaching our boys about hospitals, cancer, chemotherapy, critical illness, love, and facing difficult challenges. This was no different. It was the next step of parenting and we had to figure it out. Books helped a lot. Every night at bedtime, we read stories that gave us the words, images, and messages we needed to guide Thai through his grief. This wasn't something new. Well before Trisha and I became parents, we shared a love of children's books. When we were first married, we frequently bought books for the children we would have in the future. We'd sit in Chapters and various other bookstores, reading and imagining our children listening intently to the stories. We bought books about love, happiness, silliness, being special, and the importance of trying hard and doing your best. We never imagined that soon we would be choosing books about death, loss, and Heaven.

Most of the stories we read in the following months were from a collection of authors we knew well, like Audrey Penn and Jillian Harker. Some of the books had been Callum's favourites, some were Thai's, and others were enjoyed by Trisha and me or had been given to us by friends and family members. A few of the books we loved best had come to us by pure luck. But no matter how highly recommended or well written or beautifully illustrated, we only read Thai stories that applied to our own story and how we wanted him to think about death, dying, and Heaven. These special books helped us talk to him about loss, sadness, loneliness, bravery, joy, happiness, love, and sharing grief. They held messages and imagery that were simple and authentic.

One of our favourite books was The Kissing Hand. It was particularly useful when Thai transitioned back to school only a few weeks after we got home. A second first day of kindergarten in such a short time was going to be tough for him, but the worst part was that he didn't have his brother to talk and laugh about it with. It would be tough for us too, and we knew we needed every bit of help we could get. The Kissing Hand spoke to all of us. In it, Chester Racoon is scared to go to school, so Mother Raccoon tells him a family secret that will help him on his first day. The secret is a Kissing Hand, and it reassures Chester that his mother's love is always with him. Having Trisha create Thai's very own Kissing Hand story made a lot of sense. He seemed confident it would help.

That first day of kindergarten might have been harder on me than on Thai. Walking down the hallway towards the classroom, I relived the first day at Orde Street Public School, when everything was strange. Now here we were, about to enter another classroom. I wasn't as strong as I'd been in September, though. Neither was Thai. At the doorway to the room, he burst into tears and demanded that I take him back to his class in Toronto, where he knew the teacher and had lots of friends. I picked him up and hugged him tight. I told him the time had come to attend his home school with his other friends, but it was okay to be upset. Many things would seem unfair for a while.

After a few minutes, Thai settled down and we made our way into the classroom. We found his cubbyhole, smiled at the kids he knew who had missed him, then proceeded to the carpet to look for his name. We explored the classroom, then I found the teacher and reintroduced her to Thai. The bell rang soon after and the children located their names on the carpet and sat down to listen to "O Canada," the morning prayer, and the daily announcements. I stayed close to Thai, who wasn't ready to sit with the other children. He looked at me as if to say he wanted to leave. His eyes were tearing up and his vulnerability made me want to burst into tears myself. I mouthed, "It's okay, honey. I'm here. You're okay." I felt like I was lying to him. We weren't okay, but we had to try. Doing things without Callum was going to really hurt. My heart broke as I sat there watching him suffer.

Over the next ten minutes, I slowly inched myself further away from the carpet. I had tears in my eyes as I watched Thai hesitantly stay with his classmates. A few more minutes went by and he didn't move. Just as I was thinking that maybe I should stay to make sure he was okay, the teacher motioned for me to sneak away. She would look after things from here on in.

CHAPTER 12

Facing the World Again

After spending most days since Callum's funeral in the safe confines of our home, it was time to face the real world again. Having neglected numerous tasks over the previous weeks and months, Trisha and I made a list of the chores and small jobs that needed to get done. At the top of my list was cataloguing our family photos, which involved printing each one, then organizing them and tranferring the negatives onto a CD. I felt driven to make a second CD to keep in our safety deposit box at the bank. As I was gathering up the negatives, I found a roll of undeveloped film in our SLR camera. I hadn't used a camera in months and had no idea what was on the film. While Callum was sick, there was no part of me that wanted to capture the moment in pictures. When I arrived at the photo shop with all our family memories in hand, I asked the clerk to take special care of them. He said everything would be ready in a few days.

A second important task was writing thank you notes to everyone involved in Callum's care. I knew this would take a while, but I was determined to see it through. Trisha had always been the queen of thank you notes in our house and her reputation among our friends was legendary. She would sometimes send them in response to someone else's thank you note. It seemed a bit ridiculous at times, but everyone loved her cards and handwritten sentiments. This time I wanted to relieve her of the responsibility.

To get started, I went to the coffee shop close to our home with a bunch of cards the funeral home had given us that had a picture of Callum on the front. I ordered a coffee, sat down in the far corner, put my earbuds in, and started making a list of the people who had touched our lives in the last six months. A lot of them were professionals who worked at Sick Kids or at Kingston General, but there were also many friends, both old and new, who had helped us along the way. I didn't write thank yous to family members. Instead, they received spoken thanks, hugs, kisses, tears, and face-to-face visits.

I thanked Dr. Rutka for removing Callum's tumour safely and giving us more time with him. I thanked Sarah for her smiles and bringing Callum his favourite yellow and white-striped hospital pajamas to Toronto from Kingston, and Amy for unblocking his central line at 2 a.m. and being with me while I cried in his room. To Mariana, I wrote how thankful we were that she'd been Callum's most singular champion and protector, and to Maryanne, that she was the most special and masterful nurse we'd ever met. I thanked Zia for having the courage to visit us during those last days in the ICU and to call us at home the day after Callum died. In David's card, I expressed thanks for winning us over and doing whatever he could to ease our burden, and in Annie's, gratitude for her wonderful care and for having the humility to not always know the answers.

In the end, it took three mornings and numerous cups of coffee for me to write down all our thanks. Every day I sat in the same spot, and occasionally, when a friend saw me and stopped to say hello, I had to hide my tears. Most of the time I was left on my own. When I think about it now, it seems kind of crazy that I had to leave the house to write those cards, but I'm not sure I would have persevered at home. I also needed to prove to myself that I could do something challenging outside of the house and keep it together.

A few days later, the photo shop called to say everything was ready. That last roll of film turned out to be an extraordinary surprise, and it had me struggling to pay the young man behind the counter while tears ran down my face. In the roll were pictures of Thai and Callum enjoying the few days Callum was at home during the summer. He was bald and unwell, but his beautiful smile was in nearly every shot. Trisha had been brave and smart enough to capture some of those last perfect moments. There was Callum and Thai falling asleep against each other in the running stroller and playing together on the driveway. There were pictures of them at Callum's early third birthday party in the park, eating popsicles and cake and laughing with their cousins. Each one was a wonderful gift and I rushed home to show Trisha what she had captured.

Around that time, I started to feel the urge to exercise again. For almost three months, I'd done nothing, and even though I was physically and emotionally worn out, I needed a release. I wanted my body to feel like it used to. Since I was a teenager, I'd always liked working out, and as a dad, I especially enjoyed running with our dog at the conservation area near our home. So one day I put my shoes on and headed out the door for my usual five-mile run. The first mile felt good as I picked up the pace. My legs seemed to remember what they were doing as they moved faster and faster. By mile two, I started to feel unwell. I thought if I kept going, I'd either collapse or vomit. I felt awful in every way. I kept running, though, even as I became more doubtful about continuing. I appreciated that my mind and body were in unison – exhausted and vulnerable. I was a wreck, but I didn't care. Today I wanted to feel as much physical pain as I could. It seemed natural to want to hurt the same way physically as I did in my mind and heart.

Eventually, I was forced to stop. I cried and heaved for a few minutes, then I walked to what I knew was the most remote part of the conservation area. Standing there, I screamed as long and hard as I could, then I screamed again. The first time I screamed NO, pushing the word out with everything I had. The second time I screamed Callum's name as I looked up at the sky. Then I cursed God. I cursed the world. Completely spent, I started the jog home. I cried most of the way.

Getting to sleep that night was especially tough. I sat on the couch into the wee hours of the morning, thinking about how fragile I was. I'd been struggling with most social interactions. Going to kids' birthday parties was brutal, as was having to tell people at the grocery store that Callum had died. Even hanging out with close friends in their homes was super hard. What had happened to me? How damaged was I? My self-confidence, extroverted personality, optimistic spirit, and joy at being with kids seemed to be gone.

Crying and feeling sorry for myself that night, I nonetheless appreciated how much more I could lose if I didn't get things working again.

Later that week, Christmas was upon us, starting with the Santa Claus parade. On a cold evening in late November, there we were along the parade route, with Thai sitting in the wagon, wrapped up in a blanket. Watching the floats go by and listening to everyone laugh, sing, and cheer, Trisha and I tried to hold it together. We were determined to prove to Thai that we wouldn't let our sorrow get in the way of the rest of our life. We would suffer through anything for his well-being, and that night we certainly did.

Christmas at our house had always meant many wonderful things, as is true with a lot of families. Enjoying each other's company, eating big meals, taking time off work, giving gifts, encouraging the magic of Santa, and decorating the house were all part of what we loved. They represented the joy we felt in life, and now the joy was gone. Trisha and I struggled with what to do. We knew we had to protect Thai and our family traditions by performing our Christmas routine, which is why we'd gone to the parade. I distinctly remember going gift shopping, but in a daze of sadness. Putting up the tree was torture, then sitting at my dad's house the week before Christmas, exchanging gifts with my family, I wanted to run away. I woke up on Christmas morning and cried immediately.

The year before, Christmas had been the best holiday of my life. Our boys were so excited and happy. I had a week off work and we went for walks and played in the snow and spent lots of time together as a family. Now we were filled with grief, loneliness, and misery, and wondering how we'd get through opening presents without Callum and afterwards spending the rest of the day with other family members at Trisha's parents' house. As expected, that first Christmas without Callum was awful. I had to leave the house many times to protect the others from my fits of crying. The pain was too much to bear.

I have one nice memory from that Christmas, thanks to our six-year-old niece Claire. I was watching Thai play with his cousins on the family room floor with tears running down my face. Claire looked up at me and I smiled, but it was an embarrassed smile because I was self-conscious about the kids seeing me cry on Christmas morning. Without hesitating, she got up off the floor, climbed into my lap, and gave me a big hug, then she snuggled in close. She told me she missed Callum too, and she gently put her head on my chest. For ten minutes, Claire stayed in my arms and chatted with me about how great Callum was. She was unafraid of how her feelings would be interpreted, as only a child can be. She spoke honestly and sincerely, and gave me great comfort.

By the end of the day, I was exhausted and emotionally drained. Rather than go to bed when we got home, I decided to watch home movies of Thai and Callum. I knew this was probably a very bad idea, but I was so dejected that I honestly thought I couldn't feel worse, and that watching the boys playing together might fill me with happy memories. So I sat down by myself and started the DVD. It was a disaster. Watching those wonderful moments unfold in front of me caused horrible pain. Seeing still photos in our house was one thing, but seeing Callum run around and laugh was torture.

Instead of making me sadder, the video made me angry. I cursed the world and got myself into such a rage. I learned that night that memories, trauma, and emotions are powerfully intertwined. It was already grueling to relive those moments in my mind, let alone watch them play out live. It was too real, and left me with sensory and emotional overload. I thought then that I might never watch our home movies again.

The next morning, I told Trisha what I'd done and how hard it had been. We cried together. She understood what I meant when I said watching our home movies made everything worse. She told me she felt the same way and didn't think she could watch them again either. We sat there like we did every morning, on the couch, crying, holding each other, and trying to figure out how we were going to manage. Over the last month, we'd worked diligently to start living again. We'd gotten more used to involving ourselves in life's regular activities. But we had a long way to go. There were still so many things to learn about how to live without Callum.

CHAPTER 13

Back to Work

Moving forward meant going back to work. It was a big step. The thought of the many responsibilities waiting for me was daunting, and working again necessitated being away from Trisha and Thai for long periods of time. A major issue was that I had no idea if I was still capable of practising Emergency Medicine. Being an ER physician is a demanding job, and I was worried I might have lost the expertise and emotional reserve to care for patients and families the way they deserved. Would I be able to see patients in the same rooms where Callum had been, and interact with the nurses and physicians who had looked after him? I'd have to care for and counsel patients and parents facing life-threatening illnesses, and I didn't know if I had it in me.

With these thoughts swirling through my mind, Trisha told me something important. She said it didn't matter that I'd already spent nine years in medicine, it was okay if I wanted to start over in another field. Did I want to be a high school teacher, do an MBA, choose a different medical specialty? Did I want to take more time off before returning to work? What about working on my master's degree first and deciding later? She told me she'd support whatever I thought was best for me. She also gave me permission to fail, which was a powerful motivator for me to try again.

Following the Christmas holidays, I began the slow transition into the workplace. My first task was to start studying again. I had a big specialty exam coming up in Emergency Medicine (EM) that I had to pass. It would be the most important exam I would ever take in my life. In May, I would travel to Ottawa and spend three days at the Royal College of Physicians and Surgeons of Canada taking two written exams and one oral. Passing meant earning EM certification and authorization to work almost anywhere in the world. This was my top work priority.

The first few weeks of studying were challenging. I cried most hours of the day and couldn't sit in the same spot in the library for more than a few hours at a time. I was constantly on the move, rotating between locations. I craved open spaces and I didn't want to be alone. I listened to music non-stop, until my earbuds seemed like a permanent fixture. At first, my music selections were random, but then I gravitated towards many of the artists I'd listened to during Callum's illness. They included Chantal Kreviacuk, John Mayer, U2, and Sarah McLachlin. These and other artists, and certain songs, were vividly present in my memories. Songs like "Sometimes You Can't Make It on Your Own," "All I Can Do," "It Ends Tonight," "The Black Parade,", "Surrounded," and "Possession" spoke to me in different ways at different times, but they all communicated some combination of love, struggle, and loss.

One song, more than all the others, resonated with me in a way that continues to this day. It's "I Can Only Imagine" by the Christian band Mercy Me.

> "**I Can Only Imagine**" - *Christian band Mercy Me*
> What it will be like
> When I walk
> By your side
>
> I can only imagine
> What my eyes will see
> When your face
> Is before me
> I can only imagine

Surrounded by Your glory, what will my heart feel

Will I dance for you Jesus or in awe of you be still

Will I stand in your presence or to my knees will I fall

Will I sing hallelujah, will I be able to speak at all

I can only imagine

Listening to this song gave me hope, validated some of my fears, and reminded me that if it were at all possible, someday I would see Callum again. I would see my happy little boy, and hold him and play with him. "I can only imagine" how my heart would feel if that day came. Was there a God or a Heaven? If Heaven did exist, I could imagine my heart healing. I played that song more often than any other. I listened to it walking to work, running at the conservation area, driving in the car, and sitting in the library or the coffee shop. It filled my ears time and time again.

A few weeks after I began to study, I returned to the ER. During the first shifts, I didn't announce that I was coming, I just showed up and let the attending physician know that I'd be "helping out" for a few hours. Each time I did that, I stayed a bit longer. I was always greeted with smiles and encouragement. The ER charge nurses were especially nurturing of me. They would place their hand on my shoulder, smile, and say how nice it was to see me. They gave me the space I needed and let me work at my own pace. They often asked how Trisha was and if they could do something for her. They weren't only worried about me. I could tell that, through me, they were sending their good wishes to Trisha, mother to mother. Their looks always told me their hearts were breaking for us. This meant a lot and I relied on their quiet support much more than they knew.

Returning to the ER brought with it many patient interactions. At first, I didn't know what to expect. Would I be the same Damon as before or would I be different? I'm a chatty, extroverted doctor who likes to kid around when it's appropriate and have a good heart-to-heart with patients when needed. I didn't know if I could be that person again. Luckily, it didn't take long for the answer to appear and alleviate my doubts. I made an off-the-cuff joke with a patient and we both laughed. I smiled inside and thought, *Oh, there it is … I'm still me.* I left that shift feeling considerably more confident and hopeful.

On the next shift, something even more profound happened. I had my first meaningful connection with a patient. She was in her seventies and needed to be admitted for lung disease. She was stable and in no distress, but she was alone. Over the course of the afternoon, while I looked after her, she didn't have a single visitor. Finally, I went and sat down on the side of her bed and asked if she needed anything. She looked a bit scared, so I asked if she was afraid of being admitted to the hospital. She said, "No," and then began to cry softly. I held her hand and asked what was wrong. She confessed that she'd been thinking about her adult son who had died a few years ago from cancer. She told me how alone she felt and that she was embarrassed to be crying in front of me, a busy young doctor. We sat there for a bit. I told her that yes, unfortunately the world could be unfair, and that there was no meaning or reasonable explanation for the intense suffering that many people had to endure.

My voice cracked as I spoke, and when her eyes met mine, she *saw* me. Somehow in that moment, I could tell she knew. She said, "Oh no, please don't tell me you've lost your baby too. You're far too young. No person your age should know how I feel or be able to speak like that." A few tears rolled down my cheeks. I held her hand tighter and nodded. As she studied my face, I hesitated to say anything, but then I quietly told her that my son Callum was three and it was only a few months ago that my wife and I lost him. Now it was me who felt embarrassed. I told her it was my job to look after her and not the other way around.

The afternoon stretched on, and in the middle of the patient care area, where the beds were separated by thin polyester curtains, we shared more stories about our lives. We continued to hold each other's hand, and she said she was very happy to have met me and that I was the doctor looking after her. I left her bedside thinking I was truly the lucky one. I went home and told Trisha about this special woman who had helped me. We talked about the privilege of caring for people and the great satisfaction that can come from it. Certainly, most days at work wouldn't be like this, but there would definitely be moments to come that I would treasure. I went to bed that night with even more confidence and renewed resolve that Emergency Medicine was the right path for me.

Not everything about returning to work was helpful. There were a lot of tears that no one saw. I cried in the car on my way to work and walking from my parking spot to the hospital, which meant going through the park Callum and I had visited the last afternoon we had together in August. I passed all our landmarks: the fountain, the swings, the area where we'd had his birthday party, the maple tree we'd stopped beside to have a nap. As I left the park, I looked up the street at the hill we'd ridden down in the wagon after our banana popsicle, my heart aching. Sometimes I'd make it to within 100 feet of the Emergency Department and have to stop to pull myself together. I'd tell myself I had no business coming to work to care for others if I couldn't set aside my own troubles.

Despite my best efforts to conceal how much I was suffering, I got caught one day by my residency director. I was studying in my supervisor's office when he walked in, but I was crying at the same time, tears flowing freely down my face. I can only imagine how I looked. Actually, from his worried expression, I know I looked exhausted and like shit. He asked me if I should reconsider my plan of coming back to work and writing my final exams in May. I said a firm no to both questions. I told him I wasn't deviating from my plan, that I'd rather try and fail than not try at all.

While I was navigating my return to work, Trisha was at home by herself, and just like me, she was figuring out how to restore her former life. Being a stay-at-home mom was Trisha's favourite role ever, but now the house was so quiet. That wasn't how it was supposed to be. Callum should have been there keeping her company – playing with her, going down for a nap, shopping with her, and helping with the chores. Every minute that Trisha was at home alone was a brutal reminder of how wrong everything was, how sad she was, and how unfair and lonely the world had become.

Leaving the house was really tough at first. It brought with it the challenges of knowing what to say and how to act, not crying in public, replying appropriately to emotional questions, and trying to understand why people said the things they did. There was a big difference between someone attempting to be comforting and not getting the words right, and being stupid, inconsiderate, ignorant, or oblivious to the words coming out of their mouth. Lots of people didn't know what to say, but they showed us their hearts were with us by the look in their eyes, their body language and physical contact, the way they listened, their open-ended questions or awkward silences, or their eyes welling up with tears on our behalf.

Volunteering at school, as Trisha had done in the past, proved to be quite difficult. She came home crying and upset one day from being in the kindergarten class, not knowing if she could ever go back. As a mom, teacher, and former daycare worker with a degree in early childhood education, Trisha had always looked forward to her days of helping out as a volunteer. Schools and kindergarten classerooms were like a second home to her and she thrived in those environments, only now it was overwhelming. She still wanted to be there, but the classroom where Callum should be, the other kids laughing and playing, and watching siblings get off the bus and fool around together in the schoolyard was often too much to take.

Even something so simple as going to the grocery store was harrowing. Trisha is a very friendly, outgoing person who enjoys knowing anyone and everyone she meets. Our children, by default, got to know everyone as well. We loved chatting with the staff at the seafood counter, the meat counter, the bakery counter, and the checkout. They were friendly and had always fussed over our boys. Going to buy groceries now meant seeing all these people and many other familiar shoppers who may or may not have heard what happened to us. What was Trisha supposed to say to people who asked where Callum was? Almost every trip involved this question. It was hard enough to refrain from crying in public, but the effort required to keep herself together when someone asked that question was nothing short of crushing. There's no easy way to say your child has died.

It's not that we were ungrateful that people took an interest in our tragic circumstances. The problem was the insensitive or stupid things they said at times. I often wondered how people could believe that certain phrases, even though they're common, would help a mother's grief, like "He's in a better place" or "I guess you'll have to go back to work to keep yourself busy."

Did these people really think they could makes sense of the world with a phrase they'd read on a poster or in a book like *Chicken Soup for the Soul*? Trisha and I quickly learned that many people feel better when their life seems to have order, clarity, and purpose. These people spoke to us as if Callum's illness and dying was part of a master plan. That view made sense to them and protected them from the reality that life can be dangerous and unpredictable, and that tragic events can happen for no reason at all.

Other unwanted and insensitive questions that routinely came up were:

1.   "Why did he get *that* cancer?"

2.   "Was he exposed to toxic substances?"

3.   "Did you use fertilizers on your lawn?"

4.   "Is there a family history of brain cancer?"

5.   "What were the drugs of his chemotherapy regimen?"

6.   "Were you happy with his medical care?"

7.   "Was it so much harder because he's your biological child?"

8.   "How's your marriage?"

9.   "Are you still with your husband?"

10.   "Is it like the grief I felt when my mom died last year?"

It would have been wrong or uncomfortable to give the answers we wanted to. How do you tell people that their questions are inappropriate, hurtful, and unimportant? How do you tell them that instead, they should ask how you're doing, feeling, coping, and living without him? We wanted to say that what bereaved parents need most is looking them in the eye, and maybe putting a hand on their shoulder, and saying you're sorry for their loss.

The comments that were the toughest for Trisha were "He's in a better place" and "God has a plan" and "You're only given – or God only gives you – what you can handle." These sentiments were especially painful to hear from a priest at our nearby church. Ultimately, we felt that many of the prayers and the liturgy at Mass didn't speak to us anymore, and over time, we no longer attended church on a regular basis.

To find more support, Trisha started going to a bereavement group for mothers, where she developed a close circle of friends who she could lean on. In the first months, when she came home from those meetings, we would sit on the couch or lie in bed and talk about what they'd discussed. For starters, everyone had similar feelings. They'd all watched their child suffer and die as a result of their illness. Every mother's story was different, but there was comfort in the way their lives overlapped in terms of loss, medical treatments, challenges with relationships, and how their worlds had become so unfair. Like the other moms in the group, Trisha worked hard to move forward and restart the activities that were important to her. This included volunteering at school, going to book club, exercising at the gym, and reaching out to spend time with family and friends.

When she returned to her book club, a monthly ritual with many of her friends, hearing them talk about their lives and especially their children was heartbreaking for a long time. When the moms described their childrens' activities and their own worries, Trisha often sat silently, working to hold in her tears. Occasionally, she talked about missing Callum, but mostly she kept her feelings to herself. In her mind, everyone else's life was exactly the same and hers was dramatically different. For much of the first year, after pulling into our driveway, Trisha sat in the car and cried for a few minutes before coming into the house to say she was home.

Similarly, going to the gym again was tough, but she found a way to make it work. Although many of the people there were supportive and were mothers themselves, the environment was emotionally draining. Trisha's intent when she left the house for the gym wasn't to be on the receiving end of sympathetic questions, but to get some of her frustrations out by working up a sweat in an aerobics class, with the added benefit of exercise-induced endorphins to improve her mood. Trisha didn't have it in her to walk into class with her head down, then walk out without acknowledging anyone. It wasn't in her nature to be rude.

Over time, she developed a gym routine that let her exercise in solitude when she wasn't up to talking, and even come and go from the change room without being bothered. She started wearing earbuds. They weren't attached to anything. There was no cellphone or iPod playing music at the other end of the wire – just an empty coat pocket that concealed the jack. When she was doing her warm-up, anytime someone approached to speak to her, they noticed her earbuds, realized she was listening to music, and turned away. She then went straight to her class. She also learned to leave a few minutes early to avoid post-class discussions.

All of this took months and it wasn't easy, but slowly and surely, Trisha reintegrated into the routines that had previously mattered to her, because they still mattered.

CHAPTER 14

Hope and Reconstruction

Over the course of the winter and spring following Callum's death, Trisha and I realized we needed to make changes. Some were minor, while others were more significant. For example, the minivan Trisha and I had loved driving around town with the kids in the back had become a terrible reminder of our loss. It felt so empty with just Thai sitting there by himself. We decided it had to go. A bigger decision was to sell our house. It was awful waking up every morning and seeing Callum's bedroom without him in it. All the memories of the boys running around and the four of us being a family in our home had become too painful. We didn't want to leave the only home we'd known, but we also realized we couldn't stay. Moving forward with our life meant moving somewhere else where we could create new memories for the three of us.

Around that time, Trisha and I were thinking more about the future, particularly about unique and meaningful ways to remember Callum. We immersed ourselves in plans to participate in the Cancer Relay for Life event, coordinated an annual Queen's University Pediatric Cancer award in Callum's name, and spoke with the City of Kingston about placing a memorial bench in the waterfront park where the kids used to play. We also started making plans to adopt another child, as we'd always intended. These activities kept us busy and felt good.

My career demanded attendtion as well. I had to pass my final specialty exam. Once I received my independent practice licence and my specialty certification, I'd be able to apply for a position as an attending ER physician at Queen's University. During the last weeks before my exam, I felt everything crystallizing. My mood, despite the stress of studying, was lifting. I had more hope and could see light at the end of the tunnel. I was exercising and felt more relaxed. I even began renewing relationships with people I'd been hesitant to talk to after Callum died. Still, it wasn't an easy time. I struggled with some of the last phases of exam preparation, particularly the oral. During those practice sessions with department faculty members, I had to concentrate and perform at a much higher cognitive level than I was prepared for. Not every time, but many times, I fell short of what was expected. My mind drifted and I had flashbacks of experiences in the hospital with Callum. This rattled me a lot and broke the confidence I'd gained during those winter months of studying.

Over time, though, I arranged makeup practice sessions to "right" the mistakes I'd made. I also found ways of practising that better suited my needs. My last practice sessions consisted of me sitting at home with my dad, or on the couch at my EM program director's house, going through cases for hours at a time. Between the two of them, they had more than thirty years of experience preparing residents for their Royal College exams, so I was in very good hands. One day, Dad stopped me in the middle of our oral session to say, "Okay, we're done. No more practice exams with anyone. Save it for the real thing." And with that I was ready. Nervous, but confident.

Late one afternoon in the spring, I drove up to Ottawa to take my exams with my peers from across the country. I did my best to stay calm and focused, and I enjoyed having time to myself to get my mind into the place it needed to be. Talking to Trisha that first night on the phone, she reminded me of how proud she and Thai were that I was there and trying so hard. Her pep talk was pretty darn good and I fell asleep without much difficulty.

The first two days of the written exams went well, even though I obsessed each night about waking up on time, had pre-exam jitters right before entering the room, and fretted about not knowing the answer to every question. The third day was the oral, where the stakes are much higher. Candidates sit in front of two sets of EM expert examiners for two hours, answering a series of questions about patients of all ages with complex and life-threatening conditions. The format is fairly straightforward, but one bad answer can make you fail the entire exam, and you'd have to wait another year to redo it. Yikes!

Standing in the hallway before entering the first of two oral exam rooms, I looked down at my cufflinks and smiled. Joel, my older brother, had given them to me. He'd been through the same process four years prior and knew the stress all too well. He couldn't imagine how I was getting through this without Callum, and as only a big brother could, he decided to get me a special gift. Engraved on the cufflinks were Callum's initials. Waiting for the door to open, I felt ready, and when it did, I seized the opportunity and stepped into the room. A few days later, while working in the ER, I found out I'd passed my exams and was now an EM specialist. It was a big moment. After many celebratory hugs, I was given the rest of the day off. I went outside to the ambulance ramp and let out a huge yelp of delight that could probably be heard a few hundred meters away.

When Trisha came to pick me up, she had news of her own – we had an appointment later that afternoon to see a house in our neighborhood. Now that I'd passed my exams, we could look. Not wasting any time, we decided to put an offer on the house just hours later. It was perfect. It was two streets over from where we were living, had a huge yard, lots of windows off the kitchen, a traditional floor plan, was beside the conservation area, and was just the right size for the next thirty to forty years. A few days later, we signed the papers. It was a big week for major life events: I passed my exams and we bought our new family home.

The next week proved to be equally busy. We had signed up months before to participate in the Cancer Relay for Life fundraiser. The fourteen family members and friends who were on our team had helped with fundraising and were all coming to the event. It would be a big reunion, and Trisha and I looked forward to it. We welcomed the chance to catch up with so many people after a long winter and spring.

The Cancer Relay for Life is a twelve-hour outdoor, overnight event that attracts hundreds of participants. Team members from about thirty teams walk continuously for the duration of the event to raise money for cancer. In Kingston, it's held at the track and parade grounds of the Royal Military College, a beautiful venue next to Lake Ontario. With both uncertainty and excitement, we arrived early to set up our tent, hang our Callum's Team sign, and settle in. After eating McDonald's takeout (Callum's favourite junk food), the children in our group played on the field as more family and friends arrived. I'd made personalized team hats that went with the official T-shirt everyone got. Months before, I'd been full of apprehension and reluctance, but now I was glad Trisha had convinced me to participate. I could see that this was a great opportunity to take a step forward in our recovery.

Over the course of the relay, our team walked through the night. Memorial lanterns glowed around the perimeter of the track, music played, junk food was eaten, the moon shone brightly above, and we laughed and cried and slept intermittently. We took pictures and talked about making this an annual reunion where our family would get together and celebrate Callum's life. I thought of ways to expand our role in the future so we could generate more donations. We had a big vision of what this event could mean to us and we started making plans for the next year.

When the weekend was over, I returned to the ER and started thinking about what it would be like to practise as an attending physician and not a senior resident. Because I'd taken so much time off during Callum's illness, I had to make up six months of supervised clinical time to fulfill the residency training requirements. This meant I would take longer than normal to transition from residency to independent practice, which was a good thing. Although I'd been back at work for a number of months, I had a lot of catching up to do to feel confident I could be responsible for managing the entire Emergency Department.

Trisha and I were busy at home too. The Relay for Life had required a big expenditure of energy and time and it had come the week following my Royal College exams and the purchase of our new house. Now we had to sell our current house and plan our move, and I needed to organize my work schedule and graduate from residency. It seemed a bit crazy, but all these things were signs of moving forward, so we approached them with energy and enthusiasm. As well, we were in the midst of fulfilling the terms to create a Pediatric Oncology award at Queen's University. On top of everything, we hoped to soon secure final approval from the City of Kingston for a granite memorial bench that would go in the park across the street from Trisha's parents' house.

The bench would be a meaningful place outside of our home where for years to come we would go to reflect, meditate, cry, and be alone with our thoughts. We would sit there and watch the lake, the waves, and the ducks, and feel the wind in our hair. It would be a special place not only for Trisha and me, but for our family and particularly for Nana and Papa. Every day, Trisha's parents could look out their kitchen window and see Callum's bench with flowers and grass growing around it, birds resting on it, and people stopping to sit there to enjoy the surroundings.

I graduated from my ER residency program in June. At the graduation ceremony, I was proud to present Dr. Sarah Gander with the first annual Callum Dagnone Memorial Prize in Pediatric Oncology. I was glad to have the opportunity to make a heartfelt speech in front of the graduates, my family, the Associate Dean of the Queen's School of Medicine, and my peers, in which I expressed how important the award was for Trisha and me. It was extra special to see Callum's picture on the back of the ceremony program.

Dr. Gander received the award because of the exceptional skills she'd demonstrated with families in the cancer clinic, on the pediatric ward, and while caring for Callum, and because of the way she embodied the award's spirit. Our relationship with each other began the day Callum was diagnosed and deepened even during the ambulance ride to

Toronto. It was Dr. Gander who brought Callum's favourite Kingston General-issue yellow and white-striped pajamas to him at Sick Kids. She made a connection with us that will last forever. She was the perfect first recipient, and we had a wonderful evening celebrating together. It was an evening of hope for the future.

During that spring, I was lucky to reconnect with a role model I hadn't seen in a long time. He represented many of the qualities I admired – he was smart, well-respected, engaging, fit, and successful in his career. A few years before, he'd lost his adult son suddenly, and he and his wife knew what Trisha and I were going through. Yes, their story was different, but their emotional journey was very similar. When their son died, they'd just become semi-retired. They'd bought a retirement home and a new car, and were eager to spend time together and with their children and grandchildren. The happiness they must have felt reminded me of how content I was when Trisha, the boys, and I came back from Disney World. Soon after achieving those milestones, with so much to look forward to, my friend's life was shattered, as mine had been.

We shared an understanding that went far beyond the other relationships I had. It was comforting to hear him ask me questions that only he could know to ask because of his experience. He'd felt the same agony, and when he spoke about suffering alone, suffering with his wife, the way the darkness and quiet at night haunted his thoughts, the visceral intensity of his pain, and his attempts at controlling the all-out rage he sometimes felt, it helped me immensley. When we talked, I didn't need to ask him if he knew the same kind of grief I knew, it was obvious.

One of the most important things he told me was that my academic goals weren't selfish, rather, they were worth pursuing. He agreed it would initially be harder to recover while I concentrated on my career, and that it would mean more time away from Trisha and our children if I was working hard. But he argued that the rewards for myself and my family would be greater. He stressed the importance of growth through effort, which was the approach he was taking for himself. He talked about challenges, adversity, failure and success. Only by trying could I demonstrate to my son, my wife, and myself that I was healing.

As the summer marched on, the time came to leave the home where we'd made all our memories with Callum and Thai. We needed to start over somehow and moving to a new house seemed like the right thing to do. Our last few days there were bittersweet. Trisha and I embraced the tears that came with remembering all the laughter, joy, and love we'd created together with our boys. We remembered the night we came home from the airport with Thai, bringing Callum home from the hospital, many birthdays and Christmases, Trisha breastfeeding on the couch, the boys playing with Uncle Vico and the toy horse, Callum climbing on the kitchen counter to steal cookies, watching Callum and Thai sleep peacefully and perfectly in their beds, and so many other happy times.

The toughest of all the challenges was leaving Callum's room behind, where our memories of him were the strongest. On the one hand, his absence and his empty room haunted us. The house was too quiet and overall the mood had changed, which intensified our longing for our son and our sadness. This made everything hard. On the other hand, moving meant losing the cues that sparked our memories and maybe even their vividness, which scared us. In a way we felt trapped. Staying seemed like the safest way to protect our connection with Callum for as long as possible, but it would prevent us from rejoining life. We needed to make new memories in a new house so we could heal and grow. In the end, we were only two streets away, which to me seemed like the perfect compromise. As we packed, we held on tight to the memories we had, so they would come with us intact to the new house, where we would find a fresh start.

A key feature of the old house was the many family pictures that decorated the walls. Because family pictures were so important to Trisha and me, we were very conscious of where and how we would hang them in our new home in Callum's absence. We wanted to represent who we were as a family, but we were concerned about people feeling uncomfortable by seeing Callum's face everywhere. If left up to us, we would surround ourselves with his pictures, but we understood that wouldn't be healthy. So we chose a few special places to display our favourite ones – the front hall, our bedroom, and our family room.

On the most prominent wall, we placed the best picture of all, which is my most cherished memory of moving into our home. Weeks before, Thai, who was now five and a half, had painted his interpretation of Heaven. It consisted of a lone deer under an apple tree, with colourful raindrops and a sky full of sunlight. On it, Trisha had inscribed Thai's interpretation of his artwork next to his name: "This is a picture of Heaven… I love you Callum." Once we moved in, I knew exactly where to put it. I had it framed like the masterpiece it was, then mounted it in the front hallway on the wall above the stairs. It was perfect for so many reasons. In its simplicity, it captured our feelings of loss, sadness, optimism, sweetness, and happiness, as well as our strength of spirit. It was the perfect picture created by the perfect artist in a perfect place for all to see.

CHAPTER 15

Grief Continues

The first day of school in September 2007 was supposed to be the day Thai and Callum set off for school together. Thai would be in senior kindergarten and Callum in junior kindergarten. For the next thirteen years, they would be schoolmates, and sometimes even classmates. Before Callum was diagnosed, we used to talk to them about how exciting it was that they were so close in age. They were already inseparable, almost like twins, and now, with this first day of school, Callum wouldn't have to watch his brother climb onto the school bus alone. He would officially become a "big boy" and get on the bus with him. Instead, the arrival of the yellow bus on our street powerfully reinforced how alone the three of us felt without Callum, and that the dream of what was supposed to be would never be fulfilled.

Trisha was hit the hardest. She couldn't shake the unfairness of it all. It hurt too much. To make matters worse, it was exactly one year ago that Callum received the first chemotherapy infusion for his fourth cycle. After Thai went off to school we were left alone with our thoughts, sitting on the couch crying for Callum and remembering how sick he became that same day one year before. We struggled with the memories of the six brutal chemotherapy cycles, each one sucking more energy from his little body and causing him to vomit repeatedly. Our memories were still vivid and intense. The cruelty of Callum's suffering played over and over again in our minds. Now we were becoming angry. In the months prior, we'd been more sad in our grief and merely trying to survive, but after spring and summer had given us small measures of promise and happiness, we had more energy and strength to be angry.

Knowing everyone was worried about us, I often wondered how long I should permit myself to be angry at losing our child. How long should this stage be? Definitely a few months, I reasoned, and possibly a year or two. Maybe it would last forever. There was a part of me that thought "forever" was likely. I was aware that witnessing our struggle made our family uneasy, even though Trisha and I were trying really hard to heal. But I needed to work through my emotions as best I could, and as long as I wasn't hurting anyone, everyone else, I thought, should just leave me be. I felt strongly that no one was going to persuade me to give up my anger, grief, sadness, or any other emotion until I was ready.

Before Callum's diagnosis, I was a happy and content guy. It felt good to have close friends comment on how I always greeted them with a smile and an even temper. I was complimented for my balanced approach to problem-solving and ability to crack jokes when faced with any number of challenges. Trisha was an even happier person than I was, with more smiles, sweetness, and goodwill than most. Even when Callum was diagnosed and at his sickest, I don't remember being angry. I was mostly scared. The anger began at Sick Kids on the night of November 11, after we held Callum for the last time ... pulseless, lifeless, unrecognizable from the catheters and long illness. I remember the rage growing and feeling it inside me like a caged animal.

Watching Thai stand at the bus stop by himself on that first day of school made me want to scream. I knew Trisha felt the same. Plus I wanted to curse the world again, curse God again, and shout about the terrible unfairness of our life and the harsh reality our five-year-old was facing. That day marked a significant stage in our grieving. Even then, I knew how lucky I was. I had many people who cared about us and reliable support structures in place. At home, Trisha and I had each other, and we had no doubts about moving forward together. At work, there were dozens of colleagues and supervisors who were ready to assist me with anything I needed. We had our parents and siblings to lean on and good friends who were looking out for us. Everybody played a different role and that was exactly what we needed.

Our most important structure was the foundation Trisha and I had created together and continued to reinforce every day. This doesn't mean that relying on each other unconditionally wasn't without challenges. I wouldn't say it was hard in the sense of being a lot of work, rather, it was hard because it was heartbreaking. Trisha and I were so interconnected that seeing her cry made me cry. Seeing her angry made me angry. Waking up most mornings to find her weeping softly in another room was torture. When she told me about frustrations she was having with certain relationships, it was difficult not to internalize her emotions and even thoughts, regardless if previously my viewpoint had been different. With the passage of time, it seemed like we were the only ones who truly understood each other. Our family and friends just couldn't help as much anymore. We lost a lot of our desire to talk to people because they didn't understand what we were going through.

For me, nothing worked without Trisha. She was a part of me and I knew I was an equal part of her. I couldn't be happy without her happiness. We would be sad and angry and ache together. We would be silly and happy and joyful again someday, I hoped, but it would be both of us together. This was the only way. Right or wrong, my world and Trisha's would be the same, and we would never leave each other's side.

This didn't mean we let each other get away with stuff. Trisha was my advocate but also my toughest counsellor. And vice versa. We supported each other wholly, but gave each other a lot of tough love too. We spoke difficult truths, disagreed, argued, and pushed ourselves and each other to a high standard. Because we understood each other's emotions and thoughts better than anyone else, we were able to push pretty hard. I was glad Trisha didn't let me off the hook. She challenged me to be the best of myself and I did the same for her. We also relied on each other for advice and guidance.

Each day that fall, Trisha and I relived every moment from the year before. Between the two of us, we remembered nearly every day, crisis, major decision we'd made, and almost everything else that happened. We remembered the isolation, loneliness, fear, panic, and, worst of all, the sense of knowing we were losing Callum. As if our lives weren't hard enough already, from September through November, detailed memories played non-stop in our minds. This compounded the difficulty of getting through the "anniversaries" of what had happened the year before.

Working in the ER also had its difficult moments. Unbeknownst to my patients and most of the hospital staff, I continued, as a bereaved parent, to suffer quietly while I cared for others. Certain cases reinforced my struggle. Some of the worst pain I've felt as a physician occurred following a patient encounter I had at the time. A very sick three-year-old girl and her parents arrived in the resuscitation bay by ambulance. She was the first critically ill child I would be responsible for since coming back to work.

Over a year had passed since Callum's death and I was still haunted by his stay in the ICU. Now I was faced with managing the immediate care of this small child, including leading a resuscitation. She was short of breath, partially cyanotic (blue due to lack of oxygen), and in significant distress. Her body thrashed around as she became desperate to breathe. Her vital signs on high-flow oxygen were unstable and her parents were crying and frantic. This curly-haired, red-headed little girl needed life-saving care and I was the physician most responsible. In that moment, I forced my mind to stop sending me visions of Callum so I could focus on her. Thirty minutes later, she was stable, sedated, intubated with a breathing tube, on a ventilator, and had IV lines delivering her life-saving antibiotics and other medications. She was safe and ready to be transported to the pediatric intensive care unit.

During the resuscitation, I was very conscious of her parents, who had remained at their daughter's bedside. The nursing staff and I explained every procedure we did and medication we gave. It was definitely a challenge to manage their emotions and questions while leading the ER team, but no less essential. Once their daughter was stabilized and after I transferred her into the care of the critical care physician, I was able to step into the hallway. Keeping my composure, I walked quickly to the on-call room. I closed the door behind me and cried for five minutes straight. All the pain I'd felt at losing Callum had come back with an intensity I hadn't experienced in months. I was engulfed by self-pity. It had been incredibly hard to lead the resuscitation of that little girl, but it was my job and I had proven to myself that I could still be an ER physician. Moments later, I wiped my eyes and went back to work.

After that shift, I went to the place in City Park where we'd celebrated Callum's birthday. I sat under the maple tree and tried to deal with the emotions I'd felt earlier. I recreated mental images of Thai and Callum playing with their cousins. I allowed myself to be filled with every memory I could think of from the last time all of us were together. In doing so, I felt closer to Callum. It was amazing how graphically I could remember the people, scenes, words, sounds, and emotions from that day. Letting myself become immersed in those memories was painful, but I longed for immersion. Callum was gone and this was as close as I would get to him.

As fall progressed, I grew more attached to this special corner of the park and I told Trisha how often I went there. Before long, with the help of the City of Kingston, we planted our own maple tree in the middle of where all those memories had been created. Beside the tree, the city placed a small memorial plaque with Callum's name on it and a short inscription. Much like the granite bench across the street from Trisha's parents' house, this place would forever be important to our family. I looked forward to watching the maple tree grow. We would have picnics under its branches and remember the joy we'd felt with Callum while he was alive.

On the morning of November 11, one year after Callum died, Trisha and I felt the need to get in the car and drive the three hours to Toronto. Not knowing where else to be on the anniversary of his death, we both had the idea of returning to the place the three of us had last been together. Arriving at Sick Kids, we were grateful that it was a Sunday, which meant the hospital was much quieter than usual. Almost as soon as we walked into the atrium, we bumped into Dr. Bartels. We stopped to say hello and tell her that we were back to mark the day Callum died. It was so fitting to run into her. She was the hematology-oncology doctor who told us how dangerous our path would be, and she'd been there when we were in the ICU during those last days. I remember her comforting us and sharing in our grief. After a few minutes, we parted ways.

Trisha and I wandered through the foyer. It's a large space with 100-foot ceilings and windows everywhere. We retraced the steps we'd taken so many times, visited the fountain where Callum and I had thrown all those pennies, and listened to the Cookie Monster garbage can. Then we pointed out the window that had been Callum's and took the elevator to the eighth floor. We walked by Callum's isolation room and looked in. Our hearts ached. We then sat by the elevators and cried for a long time. That day, we sat in many of the places where we'd spent countless hours wishing and praying for Callum to survive the chemotherapy.

Later we made our way to the benches outside the ICU and sat down and cried again. Our memories were intense and overwhelming. We didn't move or speak for many minutes. Finally it was time to go. We couldn't stay forever. In my mind, I said goodbye to all the places I knew I would never sit in again. Trisha did the same. Once we left Sick Kids, I never wanted to walk through its front door again.

The weeks leading up to the holidays were a blur. Celebrating Christmas for a second time without Callum was really tough. We struggled with a wide array of negative emotions. We were frustrated and angry with our family, who seemed to have resumed our holiday rituals without a care. We felt alone and isolated in our grief. Many family members didn't know how to talk to us. More than anything, Trisha and I wanted to stay at home between Christmas and New Year's and not do anything. We didn't even want to try to pretend it was okay, because it really wasn't.

This was the first time we were having disagreements with family since Callum died. Maybe it was inevitable that some of our frustration transferred to them. We wanted them to listen more carefully and to try harder, not just with us, but with each other, with the hopes that certain family relationships would be mended. This didn't happen. Trisha and I couldn't help but feel angry that we had to put so much into just functioning, while our family didn't seem to be trying at all.

To be fair, what Trisha and I had that our family didn't was the anger of a bereaved parent. When we sat with friends who'd lost their children, they not only echoed our feelings, they allowed us to be really pissed off. Hearing that they were provoked by many of the same issues that provoked us made us feel less awful. They said it was okay to be completely furious. Their advice about how to move forward included recognizing triggers, learning to avoid particular social situations, and knowing who we could safely vent our frustrations to. Getting mad at mundane, day-to-day irritaitons was common among our group of bereaved friends. They helped us accept that the ways we were struggling were normal.

CHAPTER 16

Little Miss Mae

It was a Friday in June 2008 when we found out our life would again change forever. That was the day we received the news that the Social Welfare Society in Seoul, South Korea, had approved our adoption request. An infant girl, only three months old, had been matched with our family. In a few short months, we would be going to South Korea to meet her. The joy of that moment was tremendous. We were ecstatic to welcome another child into our family. According to the paperwork that accompanied pictures of her, she was healthy and thriving. We decided we would name her Mae, and we started making arrangements for our departure. We called our family and friends to celebrate with them. While we immersed ourselves in the moment, I couldn't stop remembering the other two times in our life when we'd felt this same degree of happiness.

Almost exactly six years earlier, we heard from South Korea that our son Thai had been matched with us. It was my twenty-ninth birthday and later that week I was graduating from medical school. None of that mattered, though, in comparison. That Trisha and I were about to become parents was far more important. Along with getting married, it was the happiest moment we'd experienced together. Then, less than a year later, we found out she was pregnant with Callum. It was a total surprise. After four years of trying to get pregnant and being told it might never happen, it happened. We were as content with life as anyone could dream to be.

After losing Callum, we believed we would never be that content again. But with the news of Mae, we both felt a surge of happiness and joy that we recognized from our past. It was one of those times that sent shivers down my spine, gave me goosebumps, and made tears well up in my eyes. Almost all the moments I'd had like that in my adult life had been shared with Trisha – our first kiss, things we did during our first months of dating, the day I asked her to marry me in Central Park in New York City, saying our vows at our wedding, sharing our successes at school and work, celebrating the arrival of our boys Thai and Callum, and now celebrating the news of our little girl.

Three months later, Trisha, Thai and I travelled to South Korea. We were excited to meet Mae, explore the cities where two of our three children were born, and learn more about Korean culture. After a fourteen-hour flight from Toronto, we arrived at three o'clock in the morning and went straight to the Social Welfare Society, where accommodations had been arranged for the week. During that time, we checked out the neighbourhoods close to where we were staying and I went on long runs to investigate further. We joined up for tours, ate as much local food as possible (well, I did), embraced every cultural attraction we could find, and bought numerous items to bring home as gifts and souvenirs. Exploring the city opened our eyes to how Trisha and I could teach our kids about their birthplace. Prior to this visit, we'd been uncertain how to celebrate Korean culture, like we did my Italian roots and Trisha's Irish/English roots. Now we had lots of ideas.

The highlight, of course, was meeting Mae and the foster family who had cared for her since she was an infant. We were accompanied by the social worker who coordinated the adoption The meeting was wonderful. They welcomed us into their home, and as we shared a meal together sitting on the family room floor, we could tell that Mae had been lovingly cared for. Her foster parents had two little girls of their own and the five of them were closely attached. Trisha and I noticed almost immediately that Mae had a very different temperament than Thai. We observed an expressive, impatient, loud, fiery, high-energy baby who was used to being the centre of attention. At six and a half months old, she very clearly wanted to run the show and wasn't shy about what she needed.

Soon the day came for us to take over the care of Mae forever. The foster family cried with us as they placed her in our arms. They were sad to say goodbye to her, but were happy for us. They knew our story of losing Callum and were glad we would have Mae to bring us joy. Afterwards, Thai told me how hard it must have been for the foster family to "let go" of Mae after caring for her. I said to him, "Yes, honey, that's why they'll always be so special to our family." I was proud that our six-year-old was taking it all in and understood the magnitude of this moment in our lives, especially since his story was very similar.

In twenty-four hours, we'd be leaving for Canada. During our first moments with Mae, Trisha and I wondered how the night would go. Thai had been an absolute dream from the beginning. During our first days as new parents, his calm disposition gave us complete confidence. This time, we sensed that our little Mae might have something different planned. True to our predictions, she screamed and cried for most of our first hours together. After tiring herself out, she fell asleep on my chest as I lay on the couch. To this day, Mae fast asleep on Daddy remains our favourite baby photo of her.

During most of the flight home, I held Mae in my arms, which I was happy to do. I was a proud new daddy and we were getting to know each other. The whole way, Thai was as good as gold, as expected. He was so proud to have a sister and was super excited when he got to hold her. Towards the end of the flight, all of us woke up and prepared for touchdown. I'd slept very little, but I didn't care. We were exhausted in every way, but crazy with excitement to introduce Mae to our family. Finally, we landed. The moment we walked through the terminal doors, Mae was welcomed by her aunts, uncles, grandparents, and cousins. There were endless happy smiles, tears, hugs, and pictures. We celebrated in the middle of the airport just like we had six years ago with Thai. And like then, other travellers noticed something special was happening and stopped to congratulate us.

Hoping to catch up on sleep when we got home, we soon realized that sleep wasn't in the cards. Our little Miss Mae, we quickly discovered, was a terribly light and fitful sleeper who didn't spend more than two or three hours at a time with her eyes closed, no matter what time of day it was. Apparently, she didn't need as much sleep as most babies, and if she was awake, she demanded that we be awake with her. Often she would open her eyes at midnight and stay up until 2 a.m., then sleep briefly and be up again until 5 a.m., then sleep for one hour, and then be awake for the day. She didn't care to nap either. The level of fatigue we felt in those first months was staggering, and we were convinced that with each passing month, we were more exhausted. This definitely didn't help Trisha and me deal with our grief and anger. We became completely run down and emotionally raw.

Not all was lost, though. There was an upside to Mae's temperament and it was a true blessing. She was exuberant and expressive and brought us great joy. When she entered a room, she quickly became the centre of attention and thrived on social interactions. She was full of hugs and kisses for everyone and was always ready to put on a performance of some sort. She was precocious in nearly everything she did – she talked and walked early and seemed to always be well ahead of her developmental milestones.

The most satisfying part of her temperament was her expressiveness. Not only did she love to give us hugs and to cuddle and be carried, she was exceptionally gifted at verbal communication. She was able to say Mommy, Daddy, and Thai almost immediately, despite not being exposed to English for the first six months of her life. Very quickly after that, she could say "I love you" and would blow us kisses. The joy these daily moments gave us made up for the extreme fatigue and frequent battles we had with her over all sorts of issues, big and small.

CHAPTER 17

Still Struggling

The arrival of Mae in our family was wonderful, but we remained emotionally fragile for a long time. For the second year in a row, Trisha and I lived through the anniversaries of every day we spent with Callum at Sick Kids. Just like the year before, we remembered him getting sicker with chemotherapy, the brief moments he spent with Thai in his hospital room, those precious times I got to bathe him, Trisha playing games with him in his bed, Callum getting even sicker and being admitted to the ICU, then living through those last days, knowing he was dying. The visions and memories were constant. The most vivid were of holding him in our arms that one last time, feeling broken until the end of time. Sometimes I thought we felt worse than the year before, but that was hard to believe.

Certainly, our second fall without Callum was different, largely because we had a new baby who didn't sleep well and was temperamental and challenging. Mae was sleeping in Callum's old crib, playing with the toys he and Thai had played with as infants, and needing to be cared for and loved in all the ways infants do. There was no escaping that the joy we felt at being new parents again was associated with the pain of our tragic loss. We cried more than we had in the previous months and it would be fair to say that we continued to struggle.

But we carried on. Faced with significant challenges, we decided to make a few things easier by doing them just the way we wanted. For example, with all of our family and friends present, we had Mae baptized at Callum's bench in the park instead of at church. I also decided not to work the week of Callum's Memoriam, both for my sake and Trisha's. When the Christmas parade rolled around, we went with friends instead of on our own, like we usually did. We knew they would distract us from how much we were missing Callum.

We said no to Christmas Mass because we thought it would be too hard and we spent more time at home over the holidays doing our own thing. We accepted that the hurt that came with holidays would be there no matter what we did.

A few weeks later, Trisha and I did our best to celebrate our tenth wedding anniversary. While our toddler and six-year-old got ready for bed upstairs,, we got dressed up, went downstairs and hosted our family and close friends for a combined anniversary and New Year's Eve party. We were surrounded by people who loved us, which made it easier to let go of feeling guilty about enjoying ourselves away from the kids. It was a conscious choice to celebrate our life, our marriage, and our family and friends. We actually relaxed and had fun for a few hours. It felt really good to be happy.

As Mae grew older, nothing changed magically. She was still a formidable child who was figuratively kicking our asses. She continued to sleep for no more than two or three hours at a time and her daytime behaviour was dramatic, non-stop, and full of defiant actions. At innumerable other times, though, she proved she could be full of fun and happy energy. There was no middle ground with our Mae. She had us on a roller-coaster ride with many daily highs and lows and really no in between. Thai, by contrast, continued to be even tempered, a great sleeper, and easy going. Thank goodness that hadn't changed.

As the months passed, Trisha and I strategized about how to get things under control. One afternoon, while Trisha's mom was watching the kids, we spent three hours at a Chapters reading children's psychology books. We were looking for anything that might help us effectively parent a child like Mae. At a certain point, we realized that Trisha had already been using many of the strategies the books suggested, as per her training in early childhood education, but with little to minimal effect. This wasn't encouraging. Then we found *The Spirited Child*, by Mary Sheedy Kurcinka. We hit the jackpot! The author describes children who are sensitive, intelligent, perceptive, energetic, intense, and persistent. At last, someone was writing for our situation. Essentially, the advice we took from *The Spirited Child* can be summarized in five phrases: be consistent, set limits, be patient, understand how your child is wired, and stay the course. This made sense to us. We were also really glad to read that spirited children have great ideas and are driven to succeed. All our hard work now would serve our family and little Mae well in the future.

When we arrived home from the bookstore, Trisha's mom told us stories about her own spirited daughter – the one I married. As a child, Trisha was confident, defiant, independent, strong-willed, and was always thinking "outside the box." Nana admitted that all the skills she'd mastered during years of teaching kindergarten were of little value when it came to her third daughter. From the very start, Trisha had a mind of her own and held firm to her beliefs. I enjoyed hearing those stories, which were consistent with the young woman I knew growing up and was married to. They gave me hope. I also thought it was ironic that our daughter was so much like her mommy, even though they didn't share the same genetics.

Around this time, I started feeling guilty about not spending enough quality time with Thai. There were so many demands in my life – parenting Mae, my academic career, my job, worrying about Trisha, trying to find time for myself – that I started to feel like I was letting him down. Thai would never say so, and to everyone else, it seemed obvious that he was doing great. He was on top of things at school, had close friendships, and was involved in various sports and extra-curricular activities. But I was aware that I was often too tired to hang out with him and do the things he liked such as play basketball, take the dog for a walk, or go for bike rides or a swim at our local pool. To be clear, the standard I wasn't living up to was my own. The effort I'd made with Thai starting the day Callum was diagnosed was unsustainable and I knew it, but nonetheless, not having as much to give him, and falling short of the standard I'd become accustomed to, bothered me greatly.

I had a hard time knowing what part of my guilt was a normal reaction to being a busy dad and husband and a doctor with an exacting career, and what part was a result of losing

Callum. My uncertainties were compounded by the many work projects I had on the go or in development on top of my ER shifts. I was involved in research, teaching, and administration, and achieving full speed was proving to be a challenge. In academia, you're either all in or out of the game. You can't involve yourself part-time or collaborate once in a while. When you operationalize ideas and projects, you make commitments to people. To not fulfill them has short- and long-term consequences. At the time, I wasn't willing to sacrifice my new desire to work hard after having been without it for so long. It angered me that my ongoing grief at losing Callum still threatened my ability to resume the life I wanted.

A nice thing happened a few months later that made me feel better. It was a Friday afternoon and I went to pick up Thai from his last day of summer day camp. I arrived early to watch the awards ceremony. When I heard the head counsellor announce that Thai Dagnone was the winner of the Happiest Kid at Camp award, I started to cry. As the counsellor explained why Thai was the winner, I could barely hold it together. Our Thai, whose natural demeanor is on the quieter side, and who behind the scenes was dealing with the death of his little brother and closest friend, had been the best helper and happiest camper all week. My heart was bursting with pride and love.

A main outlet for my conflicting emotions was exercise. Being outside, working up a sweat, and feeling the natural high from the endorphins helped keep me together. Continuing with my pattern of fighting to hold on to everything and being unrealistic with my goals, I signed up for a marathon for the second year in a row. The year before, I'd run one of the best races of my life. It was three hours of sweating, climbing hills, negotiating streams, and feeling the biliss of my solitude and being in nature. I was sure I'd had a breakthrough in both my mental health and personal fitness. But this year was different. I struggled to do the training runs leading up to the race and was far more tired at baseline.

Less than twenty-four hours after working a night shift, I woke up at 5 a.m. and drove two hours to the venue, which was basically a dirt track in the woods. As the entrants gathered behind the start line, I knew my race wasn't going to go well. It didn't. Although my time was only slightly slower than the previous year, the total amount of hurt I felt was much greater. I was extremely fragile emotionally during the race and about ten miles before the finsih, I stopped to walk a number of times. By then, I wanted to scream, cry and vomit all at the same time. I felt broken down. At the end of the race, as I got ready to drive home, I was that my whole body ached. If last year had been a breakthrough, this year was a reality check. Mentally and physically, the race kicked my ass in a way I hadn't anticipated. As I drove down the highway, I cried and yelled a few times. I got home and was sick for two weeks straight. I had to accept the sobering reality that my expectations of myself needed to change.

First, though, the annual Cancer Relay for Life was coming up. Trisha and I were actively fundraising with our family and friends. Our desire to be part of something important and raise money for cancer was still strong, and that year we were successful at raising a lot. More importantly, the Relay allowed our family and immediate friends to spend quality time together reminiscing about Callum as we walked through the night. But this was our third year and it was taking a toll. The logistical issues of preparing the supplies to camp overnight, organizing with family members who were travelling from out of town, and figuring out how to manage all of our young children in this environment felt harder and more complicated. Another difficulty was that many of the teams were celebrating having conquered cancer, while only a few, like ours, had lost the battle. The emotional hangover Trisha and I had each year in the days following the event was getting bigger.

Despite being incredibly tired and knowing we were overwhelmed, Trisha and I were thinking about whether or not to get pregnant again. We were both thirty-seven and it was now or never. We recognized it was a big decision and we didn't take it lightly. Over the weeks and months that followed, we talked about in-vitro fertilization (IVF), which the obstetrics and gynecology specialist had recommended, adding that we had a good chance of success. We also considered adopting again.

After consulting fertility experts in our twenties, with Trisha going through a year of numerous hormone treatments, ultrasounds, and injections, neither of us was eager to up the ante, which was what pursuing IVF would have felt like. We would have to travel 200 kilometres to a larger clinic where Trisha would undergo specialist appointments and the egg-retrieval and implantation procedures. We weren't convinced we were up for it. Where were we supposed to find the time and emotional strength to endure the process? What if it didn't work? Could we handle it? We weren't sure we could, given that we were already pretty fragile.

Another major factor to think about was Trisha's emotions if she got pregnant. She had loved being pregnant with Callum and I'd loved it too. She was crazy about the bond she felt while breastfeeding and all the stages of early infancy. Then Callum got sick. How would we manage if something went wrong again? We were scared just thinking about it. We felt trapped. We wanted to parent another child but part of us was afraid that we couldn't handle anything that didn't go perfectly right. We knew that wasn't realistic and talked a lot about what we were and weren't prepared to face.

Time marched on. We were too worn out and fearful to make a final decision. And then we found a solution. We decided to use the money it would cost for IVF to go on the trip of a lifetime. In October 2010, the four of us found ourselves in Hawaii for sixteen days, on the islands of Oahu and Maui, and we did nearly everything we could imagine. We stayed in great hotels, swam in the ocean every day, snorkelled, learned to surf, cycled down a volcano at sunrise, played on the beach, explored aquariums, ate delicious meals and drank fancy drinks, went to a luau at sunset, ran a race on a world-championship X-Terra triathlon course, paddleboarded and kayaked dozens of miles, took over 1,000 pictures, and overall had a fantastic time. While walking on the beach one day, Trisha and I agreed that we would let life take its course and if we were blessed with getting pregnant again on our own, that's the way it would be.

CHAPTER 18

Success and Failure

If the years between 2008 and 2010 were arduous and exhausting, the next four were a crazy ride that saw us moving up and down, forwards and backwards, often in the same day. Many things were improving in our lives, but we had a hard time sustaining momentum. We would have a big success that brought us happiness and joy, and then a setback. Life was unbelievably busy, with both of us constantly juggling numerous tasks, but basically we liked it that way. Balancing everything became the new mission. But starting to let go of things was still a major challenge, as we continued to have high expectations of ourselves.

At work, I finally requested permission to reduce my total number of ER hours each month. In fact, the reduction was small, but I felt like I was showing Trisha that with this change, our life and our family were more important than work. This resulted in a decrease in our income, but we were privileged enough that we weren't significantly affect. I was excited to have more control over my work hours.

After five years of participating in the Cancer Relay for Life, calling it quits didn't come easily. Despite our dream of annually paying tribute to Callum at an all-night walkathon shared with family and friends who brought love and support, the pressure of the event had become too much. As the captains of Callum's Team, we were responsible for the fundraising, which involved getting websites up and running, recruiting donors, and thanking everyone for their support. Although each year brought more success, which made us happy, we then felt pressure to outperform ourselves the next time. We'd also asked a lot of our family and friends over the years. Many of them had driven hundreds of kilometers after work to arrive on time, their tired children in the back seat. Together we'd survived rainstorms, biting cold, mosquitoes, and trying to stay awake all night. We also loved the venue, with its nearby lake and shining lanterns, and we'd developed relationships with all kinds of wonderful people. With so many positive memories, it was tough to walk away, but it was time.

On the morning of November 26, 2011, a Saturday, we found a bit of closure when we opened *The Globe and Mail* and discovered a short article, complete with a picture of our family, about the success Callum's Team had had raising funds for cancer care in our region. After five years, with the generous help of family, friends, and colleagues, we'd raised more than $115,000. It was especially great to have Mae and Thai see the article. What a nice way to end our association with an event that had brought us so much.

At work, in addition to caring for patients in the ER, I very much enjoyed teaching, doing educational research, and developing innovative ideas that would improve our training program for resident doctors. I was lucky to be given leadership opportunities and to collaborate with colleagues from across the country. During that period, I received a university teaching award, and was very proud that many of my mentors and supervisors from training were there to celebrate with me. At home, things were going well. Thai and Mae were happy at school and busy with extra-curricular activities, and Mae was finally sleeping at nighttime. Despite the six-year age difference, they played extremely well with each other. They loved skiing, swimming, biking, going out for dinner, visiting big cities, and travelling pretty much anywhere together. Trisha and I loved the time we spent as a family, and we couldn't have been prouder of our children.

We were having other successes too. We saw our friends more regularly, and often it was Trisha or me who organized those nights out or parties at our house. I became the "quarterback" of our Men's Night group and the party planner for a number of fun events, which included Trisha's surprise thirty-ninth birthday party, a retro '90s university kegger for my fortieth, and a costume party for Halloween. Having fun again helped us continue to move forward. And other things were falling into place. This included Trisha finding more time to volunteer at the kids' school and to coach gymnastics, me learning how to play the guitar, Thai taking drumming lessons, and accomplishing a few home improvements around the house.

Yet despite these many positives, by the end of 2012, I still didn't feel right. My anger and sadness were lessening, but I recognized a new emotion I wasn't as familiar with – anxiety. I didn't know it at the time, but my mind was overloaded with too many activities and responsibilities. It wasn't just fatigue, it was a profusion of stress. With everything that needed to be done, planned, organized, and anticipated, I had a hard time relaxing. There were too many balls in the air, and if only I could drop a few of them …. That's how I felt most of the time. I had a never-ending nervousness in my gut and was frequently on edge. I felt like I was chasing something I'd never catch. Was I too busy? Did I have too many goals? Was this just regular life stress or still part of my grief? For a long time, I couldn't put my finger on it.

The more I thought about it, the more I realized I'd been anxious since the week of Callum's diagnosis and surgery. Over the years, I'd become afraid of the phone ringing, picking up my mail, and even opening incoming emails, wondering if I'd made a poor decision at work. When Trisha texted, my first thought was that something was wrong. Was she okay? Did Thai or Mae hurt themselves? I was constantly worried about the next bad thing. This worry had been buried beneath my sadness and anger. Now that I was improving on those fronts, I realized there was a lot of anxiety that had been there all along. The struggle was still under way.

This became clear one night while talking with my friend Peter. Our families were away together on holiday, and while the two of us were up late having a few drinks, he asked me a question: "What do you want in life?" We both had beautiful families, satisfying careers, and many life successes, but he wanted to know what exactly it was that I wanted. What was most important to me? What was I still seeking that was elusive? Maybe something than wasn't obvious?

My answer was simple: "I want to know contentment again. I want that feeling back that I had when our boys were little and life felt like it should." Although Trisha and I had a much smaller home then, a very modest income, and lots of student debt since I was only halfway through medical training, I could have lived like that forever. I told him that I'd never been happier and more content than during those years. As the night wore on, I tried to explain that I was yearning for that feeling again, but hadn't come close to finding it. I'd had glimpses of it in the last few years, but then it was gone. I knew it couldn't be forced. Hopefully, it would come with time, I said. I would know it when I found it. Anyway, that's what I wanted.

It was a great conversation, and probably a turning point for me. Even as I was talking, I understood that the next step in my recovery was figuring out how to find contentment again. Success in different areas of my life wasn't enough. I wanted a happiness that lived deeper inside of me, that I experienced on a day-to-day basis. How could I possibly manage this after losing Callum? I wasn't sure that I could, but I knew I was open to it. Then a breakthrough occurred. Late in the summer of 2013, we had a wonderful surprise. Trisha was pregnant! After fifteen years of marriage and trying to get pregnant for fourteen of them, it had happened again at the age of forty. The day we found out, we had a hard time believing it. We hadn't been actively trying, rather, we were actively *not* trying. It had been ten years since Trisha was pregnant with Callum. Now here we were, feeling like another miracle had happened.

I remember how I felt those first days and weeks. Everything in the world was different. Our happiness and joy was through the roof. Work seemed easier. I slept more soundly. Problems fell away and life instantly seemed more manageable. Most importantly for me, I felt a renewed sense of fairness in the world. Nothing could take away the wounds of losing Callum, but adopting Mae, and now being pregnant again, brought so much hope. A lot of my anger, anxiety, and sadness was dissipating. I felt like I'd been catapulted to a higher level of being. The contentment I was searching for had arrived.

And then it was gone. After just a few weeks, our hope vanished at the first ultrasound. We could see the small fetus inside Trisha's uterus, but there was no heart beating. Our dream was over in that moment. Minutes later, we were crying with our obstetrician, who confirmed that the pregnancy wouldn't continue. The heartache that replaced our hope and joy was terrible. The fulfillment we felt and our contentment with the world not only fell apart, our anger spiralled out of control. How could this have happened? Why? It was too much hurt. We didn't know how we would manage the pain. Emotionally, we had nothing left. This wasn't just a simple miscarriage, it was a second chance, an opportunity to have a fourth child. How could we have two pregnancies and both end in tragedy?

It took a long time for us to recover from the miscarriage. There was no one to be angry at and all we could do was curse the world and God for putting us through such a difficult experience. For Trisha, it was even harder. It was her body that had been pregnant and that felt unwell during the miscarriage. For many months afterwards, every time she got her period, she was reminded of the pregnancy that was lost. I tried as best I could, but there was no way to take away her pain or anger or sadness, no matter how hard I tried.

More months passed, and after a lot of personal reflection, I came to three realizations. The first was that shit happens. I asked myself, *When things don't go your way, how are you going to deal with it? Who do you want to be? How do you want to define yourself?* The only way forward was positivity. Negativity would take me, and us, backwards. I decided it was time to accept defeat.

My second realization was that I loved who Trisha and I were. I loved our awesome children and our relationship with each other. In many respects, I had precisely the life I wanted. Despite losing Callum, Trisha and I had managed to find our way down the road, and I was proud of how far we'd come. We'd always supported each other and worked towards being the best versions of ourselves, imperfect of course, but continually striving. I decided to cut myself some slack and be prouder of what we'd accomplished so far.

The third and last realization was definitely the most important one. I realized that I did have the ability to feel happier than I thought. The last year had proven this to me, especially during Trisha's short pregnancy, when I'd been extremely happy. Maybe I could never have the pure depth of feeling I'd known before Callum's illness, but I could achieve a lot more than I'd given myself credit for. Despite the disappointments and heartache, I had a renewed sense of hope and confidence. I'd felt happy and content for long enough this time that I knew we would continue to move forward.

CHAPTER 19

Looking Back

After realizing that greater happiness was possible, many things started falling into place by the end of 2014. Across the many spheres of our life, opportunities arose, positivity attitudes were sustained, forward progress was made, and Trisha and I celebrated more of life's little triumphs. We were becoming more content and Thai and Mae were continuing to thrive. It's safe to say this was the most "put together" we'd been since losing Callum. Was everything perfect? No, not at all. Were we still struggling with our grief? Absolutely, but it was less severe. We'd reached a level of joy and happiness that reinforced not just how lucky and privileged we were, but the knowledge that we had the potential to continue healing.

Throughout 2015, we had a lot to be happy about. Thai became a teenager and we enjoyed watching him grow into a young man. He was developing his own identity with his friends, finding success in sports, music, and extra-curriculars, and generally making us very proud. Not to be outdone, Mae shone in all kinds of ways. Her love for school, competitive gymnastics, and life in general brought joy to all our lives. Combined with her big personality, confidence, and many talents, there were very few dull moments at our house. Trisha and I were doing well too. Because we were letting our kids have more freedom, including giving Thai the responsibility of babysitting his little sister, we had more time to be with each other. We took long walks, went on "dates," and did fun things with our friends.

Work for me had changed as well. I'd been given the opportunity to take on a more significant role in medical education, which required hard work, innovation, leadership, and collaboration. Although this wasn't where I thought I'd end up, my new academic position quickly confirmed that I'd found the perfect combination of teaching, research, administration, and seeing patients in the ER.

For me, happiness included listening to music with the kids and watching them laugh and play, being in the company of my patients and colleagues in the ER, enjoying a really good cappuccino at my favourite coffee spot, having a well-earned beer after a workout with friends, and skinny dipping with Trisha at the cottage. For Trisha, happiness was about teaching Mae gymnastics on our back lawn, the kids crawling into bed with her at 6 a.m. when I was at work, reading books to any child who would listen, Christmas dinner with silly hats on, walking at the conservation area on a beautiful day, and drinking champagne with me at home after Thai and Mae were in bed.

Of course, there were bumps along the way. There was a lot going on, sometimes too much, and we didn't get enough sleep. We faced unexpected household expenses, challenges related to having a teenager, a few scary doctor's appointments that turned out to be okay, and a work schedule for me that occasionally got out of control. But these bumps were a regular part of life and seemed to be easier to manage than before. We realized during 2015 that we weren't just struggling less, we were flourishing. This made us think a lot about our journey over the previous nine years.

I've spent considerable time wondering how we were able to get to such a good place. What allowed us to stay committed to each other? What advantages or protective armour did we have that helped us navigate that harrowing road? Could we have gotten here faster? I can't really say. It took a lot of conscious effort and courage from both of us. It was neither accidental nor inevitable. Could I have made fewer mistakes and approached certain problems differently? For sure. I wish I could have had do-overs for some of my bigger mistakes, but life doesn't work that way.

Lucky for us, we've had a lot of support on our journey. It's very likely we were more protected than most. When all the moments are added together, our loving families have cried with us, listened to us, prayed for us, had the courage to argue with us, and hugged us for weeks of their lives. Today, we remain fortunate to have a large extended family that loves us. Our parents, sisters and brothers, aunts and uncles, and nieces and nephews have all helped us to find our way. We especially can't thank our parents enough for their loving care and guidance.

Our large network of friends has similarly supported our recovery in countless ways, and the connections we've made with all of them, whether peers, younger friends, or older ones, remains vitally important to us. Our friends who are bereaved parents, whose journeys run parallel to ours, have been critical to our recovery. The ongoing bond I have with a handful of the doctors and nurses who cared for Callum, Trisha, Thai, and me has also been of invaluable help.

My medical training and career and Trisha's training and expertise in childhood development have brought us important opportunities to immerse ourselves in the mentorship, counselling, and companionship of trusted colleagues and co-workers. There are far too many people to mention, but they can be sure I remember all the conversations, tears, and hugs we shared together. It's not lost on Trisha and me that my work as a physician has brought the security of a privileged income, which allows us to explore and afford options that many other bereaved parents can't. As a result, we feel a strong pull to help others.

At the centre of it, though – what protected us most – has been our children, our marriage, and our intrinsic selves. From the beginning, nothing mattered more to us than our kids and each other. Everything started with thinking about what our kids needed, whether it was while Callum was in the hospital or those first days, weeks, and months with Thai after Callum died or the times when Mae wanted to know more about her second big brother in

Heaven. Our first priority was to take care of our children as best we could and guide them through their own grief. The second priority was looking after each other, and the third, looking after our own individual selves. These priorities, I think, in this order, are what defined our journey.

Perhaps most importantly, Trisha and I have been each other's compass and our marriage has been our foundation. Nothing makes sense for us without each other. As corny as it sounds, we've continued to live a storybook romance. Losing Callum made us more dependent on each other, not less. No one but Trisha knows the magnitude of my pain, and no one but me knows the anguish in her heart that she feels for Callum every day. I can't bear to think of a time when one of us has to live without the other. We've always been stronger together, and grieving our loss of Callum proved that. I'm a better person because of her and I'm confident she would say the same of me. Only with Trisha at my side can I function as I do today.

Something very special that Trisha taught me during Callum's illness and in the years since his death has been to have the courage to ignore the status quo and choose our own path. This came more from her actions than her words. God love her, but she never cared about what other people did, what was expected, or how things usually worked. I'll admit that her independent spirit is a large part of what drew me to her at the beginning of our relationship. Then when we became parents, Trisha made doing what was best for our children "the Gospel." Whether it was figuring out how to spend twenty-four hours a day with Callum in the hospital no matter what, putting up posters and pictures in his room, having expectations of our children to behave well no matter where we were, or driving home the notion that home is wherever we're together, her independence made me love her to a degree that I never thought possible. She taught me to have the courage to be who we are, not what others might think we should be.

I know that I contributed during Callum's illness. I had my own moments of courage, vulnerability, helpfulness, and confidence. I was afraid, yes, but that didn't stop me from being resolved to protect my family. My role as "protector" meant thinking ahead and finding solutions to problems. With Trisha's support, I could almost always see what I wanted and make a plan to help our family manage. I clearly remember not wanting to look back and have significant regrets. This meant putting Callum and Thai's needs first, before the needs of the doctors, nurses, social workers, and our own families. Knowing what we wanted and working to carry out our wishes was an ongoing imperfect struggle that meant facing our fears, asking for help, having courage in front of others while feeling vulnerable, demanding more from the healthcare system, and repeatedly digging deeper to make every moment with our children special, no matter what was going on.

Reflecting on our journey since Callum died, I'm confident we found our path back to happiness by remembering how courageous he was as a cancer patient. Trisha maintains he looked after us the whole time. When he was sick, he remained brave, happy, trusting, and, fundamentally, accepting of what was happening to him. He led the way. He trusted Trisha and me when we said, "The medicine will make you sick so you can feel better." He was very little, but he understood. Innately, he wasn't someone who lashed out or became angry or unkind. When he died, as hard as it was, we knew what we had to do. He showed us how to be brave, accepting, and even happy through great difficulty, so it was our job to live that way without him. We couldn't ask him to be so brave without being brave too when it was our turn.

The need to be brave, like Callum showed us, started on November 11, 2006, when Trisha, Thai, and I left Sick Kids without him. Many years later, in 2015, I decided it was time to revisit Sick Kids to prove to myself that I was moving forward and not afraid anymore. On November 12, the day after the ninth anniversary of Callum's death, I travelled to Toronto with the purpose of finding a measure of peace and closure. Unlike my last visit with Trisha on the first anniversary of his death, this time I had clear objectives. I was ready to take the next step in my recovery, which meant facing some of the most vivid, beautiful, and painful memories of my life in the place where they happened. I'd been contemplating this day for a long time and was uncertain about how it would turn out. While I was aware that I was being brave to confront my fears, I didn't know if I'd be able to turn a corner that day.

As I made my way from Union Station to Ronald McDonad House, I was present to the memory of each step I took when I ran to Callum during those final minutes of his life. The weather was the same as it was that day – rainy, dark, and cold. This time, though, I walked slowly and tried to remember every feeling, thought, and emotion I had as I raced from RMH across the busy intersection of Yonge and Bay to the front doors of Sick Kids, then up the stairs to the ICU, where I found Trisha, Callum and the Code Blue team. During my walk, I soaked it all in. I wasn't afraid. Along the way, I noticed the new buildings and towers that had gone up where parking lots used to be, as well as other small changes, and I was glad I could still walk unobstructed along that route.

Arriving at the hospital's front doors, I instantly recognized the feelings of fear, powerlessness, and anxiety I'd had as I desperately tried to reach Callum in time. But now, I didn't run or even go beyond the atrium. I knew there would be no benefit in going to that place of hurt where those last moments occurred.

The atrium was busy with families, parents and children, nurses, doctors, and staff moving in all directions. Standing there, I immersed myself in as many memories as I could. I was tempted to close my eyes and just listen, but I was worried I might start crying and I didn't want to stick out in the crowd. Instead, I looked up at Callum's window on the eighth floor. Our life was there nine years ago. Nothing had changed except for the absence of the stickers Mommy and Callum had put on the window during his first stem cell-transplant cycle. The elevators, the information desk, the sitting areas, the toy store, Starbucks, the fountain, and the flow of people coming and going – it was all the same. On the verge of crying, I found a bench and sat down. How I longed to be back on the eighth floor with Callum, waiting for Trisha and Thai to knock on the door, using his IV pole to push him on his scooter down the hallway, playing Hide-and-Seek in his bed, and dreaming of the day he'd be healthy enough to come home. On cue, tears rolled down my cheeks and I embraced the ache in my heart.

Moments later, I was greeted by Dr. Annie Huang, one of Callum's oncologists and someone who had become a good friend. We walked over to her office and spent the next few hours sharing stories about our lives. We gushed over our children, compared notes on our academic careers, and chatted about our spouses, but mostly we discussed the arduous journey Trisha and I had been on since Callum died. We talked about hospital systems, the very real challenges of cancer care, the benefits of learning from patient experiences, and how we wanted to care for patients and their families as best we could.

Annie also updated me on the status of the aggressive treatment protocol Callum had endured. He'd been one of the first children to receive it. She said that despite the passage of nine years, they were still struggling with how to treat his cancer. She told me that soon after Callum died, two more children with the same cancer, who had received the same treatment, died from similar complications. There had been much debate over the years by the world's leading experts, but finding a cure for this rare type of medulloblastoma in this age group remained elusive. Annie described the heartache they felt as the treating physicians. This hit me deeply. In that moment, with her words, my last bit of doubt about how and why Callum died disappeared. We'd had no real choices. Callum's cancer had dictated our path.

Eventually, I told Annie that I was writing this book and I asked if she thought other families might find it meaningful. True to form, she wanted to discuss how we were approaching the story, and we looked at many of the critical events of that time and the intervening years – our isolation in the hospital, running to be with Callum before he died, the first weeks and months at home without him, struggling to go back to work as an ER physician, Trisha's struggles as a mom, parenting our children following our loss, and much more. By the end of our conversation, Annie was our biggest cheerleader, and I left feeling inspired to continue writing.

Before leaving Sick Kids, I visited my favourite place to be with Callum – the fountain. Remembering the way we used to giggle and make a wish for each of the 100 pennies we threw in, I threw in an entire roll of nickels (pennies had been taken out of circulation in 2013) and watched them hit the water, each one attached to a wish. I remembered the dreams Callum and I had made together – the trips we wanted to go on and the fun we were going to have. I remembered his smiles, joyful clapping, and eager excitement. That day, my wishes were of Heaven, happiness, joy, strength, and that someday, somehow, we would be together again. I was trying hard to keep it together. Tears welled up in my eyes, but at the same time I was happy to think about how special life had been with Callum. I stayed in that moment for a long while, then I forced myself to let go.

I decided to sit down and watch everyone in the atrium come and go. I thought about Trisha, Thai, and our family and friends who had visited us in this exact spot, and the times when everything wasn't falling apart. I also caught myself thinking this couldn't have happened to us, but it did. As I sat there, I paid particular attention to the children who passed by, some with bald heads, some in wheelchairs, many with IV poles, and some holding the hands of distressed parents. I wished I could tell those parents that everything would be okay, but I couldn't, because for some of them, it wouldn't ever be okay again. I wished I could protect them from what Trisha and I went through and the grief we continued to feel, but I knew it wasn't possible.

As I sat there, all I could offer was my quiet support from afar. In particular, my heart went out to the kids and their families who were undergoing stem cell and bone marrow transplants in isolation rooms. I longed to visit them, even though I knew none of them. I wanted to bring them comfort, joy, or laughter, to brighten their day in some small way. In the end, what was happening to them was so lonely and unfair. It made no sense. It seemed too hard that life was asking of these children and parents to be courageous and accepting.

I could hardly believe that Trisha and I had tolerated that much pain for nine years. It was tougher than anything I could ever have imagined. To be without Callum meant far too much hurt, struggle, and loneliness. I was also aware that Trisha and I continued to dream big. We'd come to accept that sadness and anger would always be in our lives, but we knew that joy, happiness, and fulfillment would be there too. We were aiming for it.

As I write, three more years have passed. Looking back, it's difficult to summarize how far we've come. It feels like forever since we held Callum in our arms, listened to his voice, and laughed with him, and yet in so many ways, it would have been impossible for us to survive this long without him. Emotionally, psychologically, physically, spiritually, and cognitively, it's been a complex process of healing. Our grieving continues in various forms, encompassing sadness, anger, denial, guilt, joy, happiness, and reconstruction. We're still trying to fully accept what happened. Yet when I think of the life we have now and who we are, I'm proud of the both of us and excited for the future.

We love you Callum.

Daddy, Mommy, Thai, and Mae

ACKNOWLEDGEMENTS

It would have been impossible to write this book without the help of many important people. My thank yous go out to everyone, but specifically to my wife Trisha and our children, Thai and Mae, for supporting me while I wrote. I look forward to seeing our story placed on the bookshelf at home beside all our favourite authors. Thank you for the never-ending hugs, kisses, tears, laughter, and celebrations as I struggled to make this dream a reality.

To my dear friends Tara MacDonald and Sarah Stewart-Browne, who brought their editing skills to the original draft, thank you. Being told to rewrite the first ten chapters and take an autobiographical approach wasn't easy to hear, but it was the right advice. Your time, effort, patience, sincerity, and support went far beyond good friendship. You kept me honest and pushed me to write the best book I could.

To Dad, from the bottom of my heart, thank you for being a critical part of my book-writing journey through your love and guidance. For the last forty-five years, I've relied on your tireless devotion to help me achieve my goals, and you helped me again with this book, for which I'm grateful.

To all the healthcare professionals – doctors, nurses, social workers +++ – who came to our aide during Callum's illness and after he died, profound thanks. In particular, thank you to Mariana Silva, Maryanne Gibson, and Annie Huang. Our ongoing friendship is a result of who you are as people. I hope we continue to stay in each other's lives.

To the special few who had a hand in shaping the final version of this book through conversations, edits, and shared passion, thank you. You were critical to getting this book into the world.

And finally, of course, a huge thanks to everyone in our family and all our friends who have supported us over the last twelve years. We're still trying to live life to its fullest without Callum and your love helps us find our way.

OUR FAVOURITE BOOKS AT HOME

Always and Forever *by Alan Durant; illustrator, Debi Gliori*

No One Like You *by Jillian Harker; illustrator, Pamela Venus*

The Giving Tree *by Shel Silverstein*

Raising Your Spirited Child: A Guide for Parents Whose Child Is More Intense, Sensitive, Perceptive, Persistent, and Energetic *by Mary Sheedy Kurcinka*

The Kissing Hand *by Audrey Penn; illustrators, Ruth E. Harper and Nancy M. Leak*

Chester Raccoon and the Acorn Full of Memories *by Audrey Penn; illustrator, Barbara L. Gibson*

Wherever You Are, My Love Will Find You *by Nancy Tillman*

When I'm Feeling Sad *by Trace Moroney*

The Next Place *by Warren Hanson*

A Kiss Goodbye *by Audrey Penn; illustrator, Barbara L. Gibson*

Hug *by Jez Alborough*

The Very Hungry Caterpillar *by Eric Carle*

Waterbugs & Dragonflies: Explaining Death to Young Children *by Doris Stickney; illustrator, Gloria Ortiz Hernandez*

"The Little Blue Engine" from Where the Sidewalk Ends *by Shel Silverstein*

Made in the USA
Middletown, DE
03 October 2018